# Annie Oakley In Danger At Diablo

## Doris Schroeder

# ANNIE OAKLEY

*in*

# Danger at Diablo

*An original story featuring*
ANNIE OAKLEY
*of the Famous Television Show*

*by* DORIS SCHROEDER

*illustrated by* TONY SGROI
*and* HARLAN YOUNG

*authorized edition*

WHITMAN PUBLISHING COMPANY
RACINE, WISCONSIN

# Contents

*1*                                    Desert Travelers

"Steady now, Target." The slim young girl in the worn
leather jacket reined her horse to a quick stop and reached
into the saddle scabbard for her rifle. Her blue eyes narrowed as she lifted the Springfield to her shoulder and
took careful aim. This was one shot she must not miss.

On the sun-scorched desert road behind her, the small
boy on the driver's seat of the canvas-covered wagon brought
the mule team to a sudden halt and sat watching hopefully.

Twenty yards ahead of the girl with the old single-shot
rifle, a skinny cottontail rabbit bounded across the road
toward the thin shade of a clump of sagebrush. He was
small and he moved very fast.

Annie Oakley's rifle spoke sharply. The rabbit jerked
to a stop in mid-air, then tumbled to the ground.

Annie sighed and lowered the long gun. She always hated

to kill the little desert creatures, but she and her ten-year-old brother had been on short rations for several days now, and food had become a big problem.

"Good aim, Sis!" Tagg scrambled down off the wagon and ran ahead to his sister's side. "You sure don't waste any lead!"

Annie smiled down at the happy freckled face as she reloaded. "I should hope not! And when you're old enough to start using guns, you better not waste any, either. You don't always get a chance for a second shot." She dropped the rifle back into the saddle boot and started to swing down from the saddle.

She was smiling as she stood at Tagg's side with her arm lightly over his shoulders. She was glad he had no idea how close to the end of their supplies they had come. Now they could have a good meal before they went on.

As they stood there together, the girl was not much more than a head taller than her brother, though in the saddle she had seemed quite tall because she carried herself so erectly. She was nearly seventeen, and almost anyone would have called her pretty, though her features were not classically beautiful or even especially well matched. Her mouth was just a little too wide. It was a generous turned-

up-at-the-corners kind of mouth. And her eyes, set far
apart, were a little too big for her slender face. They were
grayish-blue with a few flecks of brown, and looked
honestly out of a pleasantly tanned face that was framed
by two looped-up braids of sun-gilded hair.

Her divided tan riding skirt was fringed with leather
and decorated in a neat pattern of nailheads. The worn
leather jacket matched the skirt, but it had been faded and
streaked by long days of traveling under hot desert sun.
Her homespun plaid shirt was open at the throat, and her
silk kerchief was knotted at her neck, ready to draw up
over her nose and mouth when the sand started blowing.

She was wearing a gun belt, the buckle of which was
marked U.S.A. The holster that hung from it held an army
Colt revolver, long-nosed and heavy, and fully loaded. It
was a strange weapon for a slender young girl to be carrying, even in the wide wild desert of the old Southwest, but
it was her most prized possession, and she could handle it
just as expertly as she could the old Springfield rifle.

"When are you going to let me do some shooting?" The
lad in the patched blue cotton shirt and faded overalls had
asked that question at least twice a day for the last two
months or more, and his big sister had answered it in

exactly the same way every single time.

"Pretty soon now, honey," she had always said. This time she added, "Right after we get there."

Tagg looked startled. "Honest?"

"Cross my heart," she assured him, and solemnly went through the motions.

"Whoopee!" Tagg broke away and did a cartwheel on the sand. It wasn't a very good cartwheel because the sand was slippery, but it helped blow off steam. Annie laughed and applauded. Tagg wiped the sand out of his eyes and grinned.

"Now that's over," she smiled, "how does rabbit stew sound to you?"

"Boy!" Tagg's mouth was watering already. "With onions and potatoes and no beans!"

"Why, Tagg Oakley!" Annie kept a straight face, but her eyes danced. "The last thing you told me when we started west was how much you liked beans. If I remember right, you said you could eat them three times a day and never get enough!"

"But that was two whole months ago, Sis, and we've had 'em for supper every night since, except when those miners back at Red Rock Junction swapped us that hunk of deer meat for one of your apple pies."

"Not deer meat, *venison*."

"Whatever you call it, it was sure tough! My jaws hurt for a week from trying to chew it."

Annie laughed. "I hope the miners didn't have the same trouble with my pie!"

"No fear! Nobody makes better pie—or dumplings—than you, Annie."

"That last sounded like a hint."

"Stew—with dumplings. Yum-m-m!" Tagg rolled his eyes and grinned hopefully. She laughed and tousled his sun-bleached hair. Tagg winced, but for once he didn't pull away. There was too much at stake! "How about it, huh? Is there enough flour left?"

"Sure! You win the dumplings. Now run fetch that rabbit and we'll rustle up a meal before we roll on again. I figure we still have several miles to go before we sight that stage station Uncle Luke marked on our map, and the animals all need a short rest out of this sun."

It was rough, rocky country whose giant boulders rose up out of a sandy wasteland. The only sign of civilization was the narrow wagon road that wound across its wide floor between the distant jagged peaks of the desert mountains to the north and south. There were few trees to give shelter here, although a few hundred yards away there was a stand of cottonwoods that seemed to indicate that an underground stream flowed deep below the sand and rocks.

Annie unharnessed the mules and gave each of them a pail of water dipped out of the barrel on the side of the wagon. Then she left them in the shade of a pile of boulders, and took the same care of Target. The fine cow pony drank daintily and nibbled at a bag of oats, with an air of doing it just to oblige his mistress. Annie gave him a hug and a lump of sugar before she hurried back to the wagon to start cooking their lunch.

Tagg had a fire started and was preparing the stew when she joined him. They worked at it together, as always; but it was Annie who made the dumplings, with almost the last of their flour.

It was a most successful meal, but when it was finished and the last dumpling had disappeared, Tagg was just too full to help clear away. Annie excused him and sent him for a nap in the wagon. He protested sleepily, but she insisted that she needed the exercise so she would let him off this time. Besides, he had acquired a new rip in his last pair of blue jeans, doing that cartwheel. And Annie refused to let him ride into Smoke Tree Station this evening all rags and tatters.

As she sat cross-legged in the shade of the wagon, Annie stitched and thought happily of the wonderful change these last two months of rugged travel across country had made in Tagg. When they had left their home in a small midwestern town, he had been thin and puny. She had often wondered, at first, if she had done right to start out on such a long, and maybe dangerous, trip with him. But instead of hurting him, it seemed to have done him good. He had grown an inch taller, at least, and he was strong enough now to handle the balky mules like a veteran mule-skinner.

They had met friendly folks along the way, ready to give them a hand when the going got rough. So they had had no real trouble on the road. Ten days ago, they had left the main Overland Trail, and were heading southwest across desert country on a little-traveled road. They were close to the end of the long journey now.

The desert country was not new to Annie Oakley. As a child she had lived at several far western Army posts with her father and mother. Her father, a colonel in the cavalry, had seen to it that the tiny girl was taught to ride almost as soon as she could walk.

When she was seven, her small brother had been born. The colonel and Mrs. Oakley made happy plans for the family's future. They would find a fertile valley somewhere in this new country and start a small cattle ranch. After the Indians were subdued, Colonel Oakley would retire from active service and raise blooded cattle on his ranch. The children would grow up strong and healthy. It was a lovely dream.

. And to prepare Annie for that wonderful life, Colonel Oakley had insisted on training her with a rifle and a six-shooter when Tagg was still only a baby. Perhaps he had had a premonition, perhaps not. He wanted to be sure that she would be capable of taking care of herself wherever they lived. So, when she was hardly ten, he had let her ride with his troop whenever the Indians were peaceful. And he had let his scouts teach her how to trail in rough desert country, where a broken twig or a mark in the sand could tell a whole story to the expert.

Then suddenly, when she was only eleven and Tagg was a very tiny four, their mother had died in a fever epidemic. She had insisted on caring for the sick children of some of the troopers, and had caught the sickness herself. The stunned colonel had taken his children back to the small town that had been his childhood home, and had left them in the care of distant relatives. Then he had gone back to his duty on the wild frontier—a sad, silent man.

After that, he had come to see Annie and Tagg whenever he could get a long enough leave. He had done what he could, but most of the care of her small brother had been on Annie's shoulders, and she had lavished affection on him. He had scarcely realized that he was motherless. Annie had tried her best to make up to him, with her loving care, for any lack of mothering he might have felt as he grew up.

In the past couple of years, the colonel had been stationed at a fort in the Black Hills, where the Sioux were still actively battling the endless procession of gold-seekers and settlers that streamed through their hunting grounds. He had been unable to spend time with Annie and Tagg, but he had written many letters to them both. Lately he had been reviving his old dreams of some day settling on a ranch with his family. He had even picked a site at a beautiful location on a fork of the Green River near old Fort Bridger. He wrote to Annie to keep up her practice with the rifle, and next time he came home he would start Tagg learning how to fish and shoot.

But there was not to be a next time. Instead, a letter had

come from Washington, telling Annie that their father had died gallantly while leading his troops in defense of a wagon train of settlers. He had died, but he had saved the settlers. It was something Annie could be proud of—when it stopped hurting so much.

A tin dispatch box had come with that letter. A few personal possessions were in the box—letters from her mother, yellowed and worn from much rereading, his campaign medals, and his big gold watch that he always called his "turnip." Some day when Tagg was grown up, Annie would give him that watch. She knew he would prize it above anything else, and would wear it with pride in memory of his father. The army Colt, that now swung heavily on Annie's hip, had been in the dispatch box, too.

Tucked under everything else, there had been a letter addressed to Annie and Tagg: *To be read in case of my death.* In his letter the colonel instructed them briefly: *Get in touch with your mother's brother, Luke MacTavish, in a town called Diablo in the southwest part of the Indian Territory. He is a sheriff there, and a good substantial citizen. I am sure he will be glad to open his home to you both.*

It was only at the end of his rather curt note that the colonel allowed himself to express some of the love that he had for his motherless pair. He was not accustomed to soft words, even on paper they sounded awkward and ill-at-ease: *Annie, keep on taking good care of your brother until the day when he is grown and can take his place as your protector. You have done an excellent job. If God wills that I do not see you again, I want you to know that I have always been proud of you both. Your affectionate father, Jared Oakley.*

When the first shock was over, Annie had taken stock of their situation. Their father's relatives could not keep them on there, and Annie had no way of making a living for herself and Tagg. Tagg had taken the loss of their father hard, and had grown thin and pale. Nothing seemed to interest him. Annie decided it was high time to write to their uncle at the strange-sounding town in the Territory.

Her letter brought a quick reply. Uncle Luke was delighted to have them come and live with him. He sent money and a map he had drawn of the long road they would have to travel to get to Diablo. He urged them to start as soon as they could find someone reliable to travel with. Annie had tried to find a party going west, but no one seemed to want to be burdened with a young girl and a small boy. So at last they had cheerfully started out alone,

with a span of mules to pull their wagonload of household
goods and supplies.

They had taken turns riding Target and driving the
wagon all the way across country. Their map had not proved
to be as accurate as Uncle Luke must have thought when
he sent it to them. He had left out several high mountain
ranges and a couple of wide rivers! But Annie didn't blame
him too much. She knew he had based the map on reports
from many travelers, and it was natural that they would
remember the details differently. On the whole, though, .
the map had helped a lot. And now, on the last leg of the
journey, the map covered ground familiar to the sheriff
himself, his own county, and she knew she could rely on it.
*Turn here,* he had penciled at a dot marked, *Smoke Tree
Station. Diablo 15 Miles S. W. by Stage Road.* So with any
luck, they would soon be there.

A light breeze was flapping the canvas that stretched
over the furniture in the wagon. A faint distant rumble
came from the mountains that fringed the wide valley floor.
Annie noticed with a start that the sun was already half
down the sky. And Smoke Tree was still miles off.

She stared anxiously at the mountains. Huge fluffy
clouds, like giant puffs of whipped cream, hung over the

jagged peaks of the highest range. Their billowy tops were snowiest white, but down below they were a dirty gray, and she could see forked flashes of lightning there. The crash of thunder was louder now and more frequent. She thought uneasily of the giant cloudbursts that sweep down the barren sides of the desert mountains, to roll in a terrifying wall of water across the flatland, carrying a wildly tumbling mass of uprooted trees, great boulders, and sand with it. Not even the strong mesquite and the spiked cactus can stand against the dreaded flash flood, and there is no way of knowing when it will come roaring down and what direction it will take.

This particular storm might not mean danger, but she had no intention of waiting there to find out. She gently shook Tagg awake. While he was rubbing the sleep out of his eyes, she brought the reluctant mules and started to harness them.

"While I hitch up," she suggested briskly, "why don't you trot over to those cottonwoods and see if you can pick up some kindling? We've used up all we had in the wagon."

"Sure, Sis!" Tagg was ready any time to explore new places.

"But hurry!" she warned. There was no use mentioning

the storm in the mountains. They would be out of its path in a short time if they started moving soon. "And if you don't find any right handy, come back. I want to get rolling so we can be at Smoke Tree Station before dark."

Tagg was already loping off toward the stand of cottonwood trees a few hundred yards away. Annie turned back to the balky mules. "I know," she told them, "it's a lot nicer sleeping in the shade than pulling this heavy load. But you'd be a heap more uncomfortable if you got in the path of a big, husky flash flood!" And she backed them firmly into their harness.

Target was pulling at his rope when she went over to saddle him. She fed him a lump of sugar from her pocket and scratched his ear. Target nuzzled her and whinnied affectionately. Then he snorted suddenly and gave her a nudge with his nose that nearly knocked her hat off. "Okay," she laughed, "I can take a hint." She untied his hitch rope and started to throw on his saddle. "And don't act so innocent. I know you did that to hurry me!"

She had the saddle in place and was tightening the cinch when she heard Tagg calling excitedly. His voice was faint in the distance: "Hi, Annie! Come see what I found!"

She looked toward the cottonwoods, but he was not in

sight. There was a low sandhill beyond them. She swung lightly into the saddle and stood in the stirrups to look over it. Now she could see him. He was bending down to study something in the sand, but what it was she could not make out at that distance.

She chuckled to herself. Tagg was always making some big discovery on this trip. Sometimes it was a centipede or a shiny millipede with all his legs going at once as he tried to get out of the reach of a small curious boy. Sometimes it was only a small chuckwalla lizard blinking at him from a rock or scuttling away fast over the hot sand. Once Tagg had grabbed for one of them and caught it by the tail. To his horror, the tail came loose in his hand, and the chuckwalla kept on going. Tagg was very near tears that day, thinking he had injured the little fellow beyond repair, but Annie explained that a new tail would grow in place of the one he had pulled off.

Whatever it was that Tagg had discovered this time, he was very excited about it. He was scrambling to his feet, and starting off on a run toward a mesquite thicket a few yards beyond. Annie started up Target and headed after him. Halfway there, she cupped her hands around her mouth and called, "What are you after?"

Tagg paused and looked back. "Dunno yet," he yelled. "I'm trailing it! Come on!" He started off again.

Now he had reached the thicket and was pushing through. She could see that he was standing close to the edge of a deep, rocky ravine which she had not been able to see before.

"Take it easy there!" she called, but Tagg grinned back and waved, and then started down out of sight.

She pulled up where he had been bending to study the ground, and saw the mark that had excited him. It was a curious S-shaped trail in the soft surface of the sand. Along the curve of the S, the sand was ruffled as if a piece of rope had been looped and dragged heavily across it. The strange mark was repeated many times between here and the edge of the ravine. Somewhere a long time ago, she had seen a trail like this. And for some reason the sight of it now sent a cold shiver down her spine.

It was connected with something scary—but what? She hastily tried to recollect. Her father had taken her for a walk on the desert, she remembered. She had run ahead through the sand to pick some wild flowers for her mother. Her father had shouted something, and then he had fired his big pistol. She remembered that the smoke got in her

nose and made her sneeze when he picked her up in his
arms. Then he had shown her that mark in the sand. And
he had said—suddenly she remembered what it was he
had said!

"Tagg!" Her voice sharpened to a scream. "Tagg! Come
back!" There was no answer.

She prodded the surprised Target into a run across the
soft sand. He floundered and snorted indignantly as it gave
way beneath his hoofs. But Annie, with voice and slapping
rein, urged him on desperately, and somehow he managed
to find his footing again and ran.

She had not reached the edge of the ravine when she
saw Tagg. Apparently he had slipped as he started to climb
down. He had stopped his fall by clutching the projecting
roots of a sturdy mesquite. Now he hung there, only a foot
or two down, gripping it with both hands. To let go would
mean a plunge of twenty feet to the rocky floor. But why
didn't he try to pull himself up? she wondered. Then she
saw!

Coiled on a flat rock that jutted out from the side of the
slope, was the desert creature whose odd trail he had followed—a horned rattlesnake. The sidewinder was drawing
its ugly head back above tightly wound coils, its slitted eyes

fixed on the boy's white face. In another moment it would strike.

Annie had no time to stop to take aim. Without slackening her speed, she made a lightning-fast draw and pulled the trigger of the heavy Colt.

Her shot smashed the reptile's head from its body. A second shot swept the writhing coils off the ledge and down into the ravine.

She pulled to a sliding stop a few feet from the edge, and threw herself off the pony, smoking revolver in hand. As she ran, she called, "Hang on, Tagg! Hang on tight! I'm coming!"

Tagg hung on. He had no intention of letting go and maybe dropping down into the ravine with the dead snake. He remembered hearing that snakes usually go in pairs. Its mate might be waiting down there.

Annie knelt at the edge and reached down to grasp Tagg's wrist, while he scrambled to get a foothold among the loose rocks. She braced herself and hauled hard.

In a few minutes he was safely up over the edge and sprawled breathless on the ground. As soon as she was sure he had not been hurt, Annie stood off and looked him over disgustedly. "Of all the silly tricks!" she began. "Look at

you! You've torn your shoe. And that's a bad rip in your
shirt sleeve! Well, this time you'll just mend it yourself,
young man!"

She was mad, all right, he decided. He was still a little
shaky as he got to his feet and tried to brush off the dirt. He
avoided meeting Annie's accusing eyes. She pointed to the
wagon standing away back on the road.

"Taggart Thompson Oakley," she said sternly, "get back
on that wagon this minute. And if I ever catch you trailin'
a sidewinder again, I'll—" she broke off suddenly, reached
out and grabbed him in a big hug. Tagg squirmed and
protested but she held him tightly a moment. That was a
close call he had had—much too close.

"Aw, Annie! Let go!" One minute she was scolding
and the next she was hugging. Tagg much preferred the
scolding.

Just as suddenly as she had hugged him, she let go and
gave him a good strong shove toward the wagon. "Scoot!"
she said cheerfully, "and next time you're sent on an errand,
don't wander off on any side trails. They usually get folks
into trouble!"

Tagg grinned back at her. "I promise, Annie. And
thanks for being the best shot in the world!"

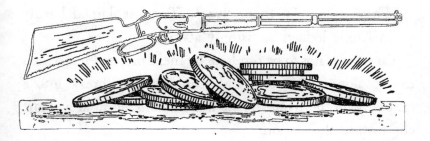

## 2          Smoke Tree Station

The sun was sliding down out of sight over the edge of
the western desert, as Annie and Tagg came in sight of
Smoke Tree Station. It was only a handful of squat buildings huddled at the foot of a sunbaked hill, but it was a
welcome sight to the tired travelers.

Tagg whooped happily. "We'll be there in ten minutes!
Watch me go!" He laid the whip to the jogging mules.

"Hey! Stop that!" Annie called back reprovingly. "Easy
does it, young feller! Those poor things are as anxious to
get there as you are, but we're not going to run their hearts
out just to save a few minutes. Slow down!"

Tagg knew she was right. He slackened the reins, but
the mules just flicked their long ears and kept on at a faster
pace. They were hungry, and their good mule-sense told
them that water and food were close at hand.

"They're doing it themselves!" Tagg explained hastily when Annie looked accusingly at him.

Target was not to be outdone by mere mules. He decided to step along faster, too, and Annie let him break into a canter. Soon the whole outfit was moving along at a smart clip toward the station.

"Look, Annie!" Tagg was pointing off to the south as he called to her. A tiny puff of dust had appeared in a gap between the hills. It was moving rapidly along what must be a winding road. "What's that?"

Annie studied it. "It seems to be some kind of a four-horse wagon. Why, it's a stagecoach! I can see it now. It's headed toward the station!" As she spoke, they both heard distant sharp reports.

"Sounds like they're shootin' off firecrackers!"

Annie shook her head. Her face showed she was worried. "Gunfire!"

Tagg jumped up on the seat of the wagon and shielded his eyes against the setting sun. "Indians?" He sounded as if he hoped so.

"I doubt it." She had wheeled Target and was riding close to the wagon. Without realizing it, she rested her hand on the Colt in her holster. She spoke lightly, "Uncle Luke wrote that there aren't any hostile Indians around here. They're mostly all on the reservations, and he says they're living up to the Treaty now that their old leaders are in prison or reformed." '

Tagg couldn't help being just a bit disappointed. An Indian raid just as he and Annie reached the safety of the stage station would have made something to write about to his old friends back home.

"Anyhow, whatever the shooting meant, it seems to be all over now." Annie smiled.

"Maybe whoever was chasing the stage gave up when they got in sight of the station," Tagg guessed. "Too bad we weren't closer. We might have got in on it."

"Be glad we didn't! Don't be so bloodthirsty, young punkin!" She laughed, and then added, "Probably was some cowboy passenger celebrating pay day. I remember when Mother and I were with Dad, at Fort Apache, we had a house at the edge of town for a while. And on Saturday nights when the ranch hands got paid, they came to town to let off steam. The merchants boarded up their windows and we all stayed indoors. After they'd spent their money, the cowboys would ride up and down just firing their guns in the air. Mother and I would hide under the bedcovers!"

Tagg chuckled. "Wouldn't have scared me!" he boasted.

Up ahead, the stage was approaching the station. The thick-timbered gate in the adobe wall was swinging open. Annie could see men running out to meet the stage, waving their arms in excited greeting. Then the stage rocked into the station yard, and the men at the heavy gate started to swing it shut.

Annie fired three times into the air, in rapid succession. One of the men at the gate stared in their direction, then waved an arm in reply, and swung the gate wide open again. The mules stepped out briskly, and Target cantered as gaily as if they had not covered twenty miles since breakfast. It was all Annie could do to keep the hungry animals from galloping the last few hundred yards.

Tagg straightened his shoulders and sat up erect as he handled the reins with a flourish. Annie cast a quick glance back at him and smiled secretly. Tagg always made a good entrance, just in case there were other small boys somewhere around to be impressed. Tagg caught her look and grinned in reply. He knew he never fooled Annie very far.

"Bet we'll find a lot of people here who know Uncle Luke," he called over the rattle and squeak of the wheels.

"I should hope so," she called back, "seeing he's been

their sheriff for the past five years!"

The short desert twilight was already fading into darkness when they reached the gate a few minutes later. As they moved into the big square unloading yard, Annie took a quick look around. If there were several wagons under the sheds, it would mean that the station was crowded. In that case, she and Tagg might have to camp outside the walls tonight.

To her relief there were only an old buckboard and a buggy in the sheds, evidently belonging to the station itself. Over in front of the big rambling adobe headquarters building, the stage was unloading an excited trio of passengers. Several men in typical Western garb had gathered to greet them, and a tall thin man in shirt sleeves hurried out of the building as she watched. He must be the superintendent of the station, she guessed, from the way he took charge and led the agitated passengers into the building.

The man who had swung the gate open for her closed it now and dropped the heavy iron bar across it. He picked up a lighted lantern and handed it up to her.

"Here y'are, ma'am," he said briskly, then pointed toward the stables across the wide yard. "You'll find plenty

of room for your critters. Help y'self to the feed an' water."
He started to move away hastily toward the others.

"We've come a long way today," Annie called after him,
trying to sound cheerful, "and we'd like somebody to give
us a hand."

"Be glad to help, ma'am, soon as I git back!" He
retreated quickly before she could argue him into giving up
the excitement of what was going on over at headquarters.

"Was it a real holdup?" Tagg called from the wagon.
"Did somebody shoot at them?"

"He didn't give me time to ask!" Annie answered wryly.
"We'll find out all about it when—and if—he comes back.
Meantime we'll start unharnessing."

The stables were big and roomy. Annie found clean stalls
for all three of her animals, and a good supply of water
and feed. Tagg, as usual, did his full share of the work,
even if he did grumble a few times, "Wish that fellow'd
come back and tell us what happened."

But they were still alone when they finished taking care
of the mules and Target, and they started over to the main
building carrying their carpetbags. Annie slung her saddle
over her shoulder. There was always a chance in any
strange place that someone might switch saddles, and hers

was an especially fine tooled leather one, one of her father's last gifts to her.

They could hear excited voices through the open door of the headquarters adobe. The square blob of light from inside the room outlined a man's figure as they came up. It was the man who had left them at the gate. He saw them and stopped abruptly.

"Dawgone, ma'am, I'm sorry! I plumb forgot you folks in all the ruckus here!"

Tagg couldn't hold back. "Was the stage really attacked?"

"Sure was! About two miles out. Coupla fellers popped outa the big rocks at the Bend and threw down on Zeke. He's the driver. He ain't the kind to argufy with a six-gun, so he pulled away pronto and reached for the sky. They spilled them passengers out alongside the road, roughlike, and lined 'em up. But they didn't hurt nobody. They jist took their val'ables and cussed 'em out because they wasn't carrying much coin. Then they rode off."

Tagg was disappointed. "But we heard the shooting!"

"That was Zeke signalin' the station he'd run into trouble."

Tagg thought it was high time to do a little bragging.

"Huh!" he snorted, "it's a good thing for those outlaws they didn't try to stop *us!* Annie would've sent them flying!"

"Yuh don't say!" The stableman laughed and winked at Annie over the boy's head. "She don't look so fee-rocious to me!" Then he sobered. In the lamplight from the open door, he noticed for the first time that she was young and pretty. "If I was you, miss, I wouldn't try to do any more travelin' around here alone. We're havin' more'n our share of outlaw trouble these days."

"Thanks for the advice." Annie smiled at him.

The man pointed his thumb over his shoulder at the open door. "The long skinny feller behind the counter is Jim Castle. He's boss of the station. You take his advice and you'll be okay."

He disappeared into the darkness toward the stables, and Annie led Tagg inside the headquarters building. The big main room was warm and inviting after the chill of the desert night air. Its great stone fireplace was piled high with blazing juniper logs, sending a faint pleasant perfume through the room as tiny spirals of smoke stole up along the massive face and were lost in the blackened beams. Several colorful Navaho blankets were hung on the walls, while others carpeted the rough plank floor. A huge wagon wheel hung down horizontally from the center of the ceiling, a bracket at the end of each spoke holding a lighted oil lamp with a brightly polished brass reflector. Tagg could hardly take his eyes off its dazzling splendor.

"Wow-ee!" he breathed, "look at that, Annie!"

But Annie's attention was centered on the group gathered at the long counter at the far end of the room. The tall thin man behind the counter was undoubtedly the superintendent that the stableman had referred to. Glaring up at Jim Castle was a small, stout, red-faced man in a tall beaver top hat and a plaid English traveling cape of fashionable cut. He carried an ivory-headed cane with which he pounded the counter.

"What are you going to do about this outrage?" he was barking angrily.

The lanky superintendent shook his head mournfully and pulled at a limp mustache that drooped almost to his chin.

"Nothing we can do about it tonight, sir. But first thing in the morning—" He broke off to turn to the stage driver who was standing by. "How about it, Zeke? Did you see their faces?"

"Nope," said Zeke unhappily. "They were wearing hoods made out of horse blankets."

"Which same they've chucked in some gully by now," put in one of the listeners. The others nodded agreement.

"I wouldn't mind so much losing my money and my watch," the traveler complained. "But those desperadoes took my sample case, and I can't do any selling."

"What's your line, mister?" It was the same cowboy who had spoken before.

"Imported perfumes, sir! Rare French extracts used by the cream dee la cream of society in salons from coast to coast!"

"Do tell!" The cowboy was puzzled. "I been in a heap of saloons, but I'm blamed if they smelt like cologney!"

"My good fellow, I said salons, not saloons!"

"Well, whichever, it seems like the best way to catch them road agents is to keep sniffin' around till we find a couple of hombres that smell too pretty!"

Several of the hearers snickered and the traveling man's face turned a brighter red. Over at the fireplace, Tagg giggled and nudged Annie, but she hastily laid her hand over his mouth. "Sh-h-h!" she warned. The superintendent was speaking.

"The nearest peace officer's at Diablo," he was saying soothingly. "I'll send off word to him in the morning."

Tagg whispered excitedly to Annie, "Is he talking about Uncle Luke, do you think?"

She nodded and smiled. "Of course! There's only one sheriff in a county!"

Her smile faded suddenly as the traveler's voice whipped sharply across the room. "Why tell him something he knows all about now?"

"Meaning what?" Castle's voice sounded hard and dry.

"You live around here. You know what everybody in Diablo says about him and his kind of law enforcement!"

# 3         Gossip or Truth?

The words of this angry traveler struck Annie with shocking force. She gasped involuntarily as she realized that he was openly accusing her uncle of dishonesty. Tagg turned to her with a puzzled frown.

"What's he saying about Uncle Luke?"

She shook her head at him and whispered, "Let's listen."

Over at the counter the tall superintendent was speaking quietly. "You've been talking to the wrong people in Diablo, mister. Sheriff MacTavish is an honest man and a good law officer. Anybody that holds a job like his is bound to have enemies, even among the folks he does the most for."

"Then why doesn't he jail some of the riffraff that infest his territory? Like those two toughs that robbed me just now? Is he scared—stupid—or crooked himself?" The stout man was getting more sure of himself by the minute, as he saw approval in the eyes of several of his listeners. "I'll tell you what I think—" he began. He stopped abruptly as he saw the look on Jim Castle's face. The tall man was looking at him with the expression of a St. Bernard dog watching a tumblebug, and with just as little respect. He flushed uncomfortably and held his tongue.

"I don't know why I'm botherin' to explain," Castle spoke slowly and carefully, weighing his words, "but you've got a wrong slant on things from somebody. This is a big stretch of country, and Luke's got just one regular deputy hired to help him. Those two can't be all places at once, but they do their all-fired best! And any honest citizen of this county'll back me up on that!"

From her place by the fire, Annie studied the faces of the men at the counter. A couple of local men nodded agreement with the station manager, but others looked blank or turned away with an obvious attempt to avoid being drawn into the argument. It was plain to Annie that there was a difference of opinion here about her Uncle Luke. A disturbing difference.

She listened tensely as the pompous little man began to speak again.

"The person who told me about MacTavish happens to be a very substantial citizen of Diablo. And he says that either your sheriff is afraid to bring the law on the ruffians who have been robbing travelers like ourselves, breaking into your local bank, and stealing mine payrolls from decent mine owners, or *he's in with them!*"

Tagg jumped to his feet and started over to the group. Annie caught his arm. "Wait!" she warned him.

"But, Annie! Didn't you hear what he said about Uncle Luke? I'm going to tell that mean old man—"

"Wait, honey. That won't help. Let's hear what Mr. Castle has to say to that."

For a moment, Jim Castle was silent. The others watched him. When Castle spoke, it was with a good-natured chuckle. He even smiled down at the traveler. "Folks who spend a few days here and a few days there hear a lot of things. Sometimes they're true. Other times they're just something spilled out of a bottle on a hotel bar." He turned and included them all in one broad gesture. "In any case, arguin' about the sheriff won't get us anywhere tonight. It's time I was giving you folks a chance to turn in and get a good night's rest. Now if you'll just sign your name and town in the book—" he smiled as he pushed the register toward the nearest of the stage passengers.

The stout traveler glowered, but as he looked around for some encouragement to continue the argument, he saw that Castle had taken their minds off the subject. He might as well keep quiet. But he made a mental note that the stage company would get a letter from his lawyers, insurance or no insurance. He would collect plenty.

Over at the fireplace, Tagg grinned at his sister. "I guess that settled Mister Big Talk!"

She nodded and smiled faintly. She was watching the little group of men break up. Some of them followed an old Mexican servant away toward the sleeping quarters down the hall. Others drifted out the front door. They were the hardy souls who lived in the open and scorned the confines of a room at the station. The sky was their familiar roof and they preferred it so.

Annie was troubled. Gossip or not, the salesman's angry words against her uncle remained in her mind and bothered her. She had never worried, in all the long weeks of her journey with Tagg to this new country that was to be their home. She had felt able to handle any situation that came up along the way, or to find a helping hand if it was too much for her, alone. But the thought that her uncle might not be all she expected was a new and alarming one.

She knew that her father had not seen Luke MacTavish for years. Probably not since her mother's funeral, when Tagg was a baby. She had only the dimmest remembrance of him there. His letter in answer to hers had been warm and friendly; he had assured her that she and Tagg would be happy on his "Bull's-Eye Ranch." He had told them he would have a pony for Tagg, and he was buying a new wood stove from the mail order catalogue so that Annie would find the cooking easier. There had been nothing in his letter to hint that he did not really want them to come and make their home with him. If it was true, as the sales-man had said, that he was friendly with outlaws, he cer-tainly would not have invited them. They would be sure to get in the way. Or—Annie had a sudden sinking feeling—would he be able to fool people better if he had them living there?

She felt that she must know more about Luke MacTavish before she and Tagg reached his ranch and settled into being his "family."

"Come on!" She pushed her wide-brimmed hat back off her forehead and picked up her saddle. Tagg valiantly

struggled with the carpetbags as they moved over to the
counter. "Let's find out where we sleep tonight," she said
cheerfully. "Looks like everybody else is taken care of."

Jim Castle was alone behind the counter as they came
up. He was startled to see a young girl and a sleepy-eyed
boy. He had not noticed them before. "Where on earth did
you two kids drop from?" he demanded. "And where are
your folks?" He looked past them at the open door.

Annie smiled and held out her hand. "Our name is
Oakley," she said. Castle looked puzzled, but he took the
hand politely.

"Oakley," he repeated. There was something familiar
about the sound of it. "Oakley?" He still held her hand,
absent-mindedly. Suddenly he gripped it harder, and shook
it vigorously. "Why, sure! Now I recollect! You must be
Luke's kids that he's expecting, Annie and Tagg Oakley!"

"I'm Tagg and she's Annie!" Tagg pointed earnestly.

"I almost figured that out for myself!" Jim Castle
chuckled down at them, his long mustache dancing as his
mouth widened in a friendly grin. "I'm sure glad you got
here. Luke's been fussing worse'n an old biddy hen settin'
on a china egg, because you took so long."

"I'm glad to know Uncle Luke has a friend like you,

Mr. Castle." Annie spoke soberly. "We heard what that man from the stagecoach was saying about him."

"Oh!" Jim Castle hesitated the smallest fraction of a minute, but Annie noticed it. "Tell you what I really think," he told her. "That traveling man was most likely flashing his fat bankroll around in Diablo last night, and a couple of his so-called pals followed the stage and took it away from him!"

"But he said the man he talked to about Uncle Luke was a prominent citizen—"

Castle laughed, and dismissed the prominent citizen with a scornful wave of the hand. "That might be true, too. There's a thing called politics that makes some folks run off at the mouth. And we're having an election soon. So don't pay any attention to that."

Tagg was rubbing his eyes sleepily. Annie put an arm across his shoulders. "This colt needs a place to bed down, Mr. Castle. If you'll tell me where to put him, I'll be much obliged."

"I can give you a couple of rooms on the side away from the stables." He watched her sign the register. "I figured one of them for that traveling salesman, but I changed my mind when he started blowing off about Luke. I gave him

one on the side with the flies. He won't get much sleep after daybreak!"

Chuckling, he led them down the corridor to their rooms, followed by the old Mexican servant with their bags and Annie's saddle.

The tiny rooms were only a few feet square, but they had good pole beds, laced with thick strips of rawhide, and raised off the hard, dirt floor. The guest was supposed to supply his own blankets, as well as a luxury item called towels. But there was a strong roof overhead, and a warmth that still lingered inside the thick adobe walls, a reminder of the desert day just past and the one to come.

"We'll be pulling out early in the morning," Annie told Jim Castle. "I want to get to Diablo before dark."

"Well, now," he patted Tagg's sleepy head, "I don't guess you'd better, Miss Annie. I'll send word to Luke you're here, and in a couple of days he'll come get you. It won't hurt the young 'un here to have a bit of rest."

Annie started to protest, but the superintendent didn't wait to listen. He said good night to them briefly, and went out, closing the door.

"Off to bed you go!" she told Tagg cheerfully. Without protest he took the lighted candle she gave him, and went to his room. A few minutes later, she heard the pole bed squeak, and saw that the candle was out. As soon as she was sure he was asleep, she tiptoed in and tucked the blanket securely around him, touched his forehead lightly with her lips, and then stole out.

Later, while Tagg slept soundly, she sat for hours staring out through the narrow loophole windows in the thick adobe wall of her room, thinking over what she had heard about her uncle and trying to decide what it would be best to do. Across the moon-drenched stillness of the desert, she heard a coyote howl mournfully. Nearer at hand, as if in answer to his challenge, the horses snorted and stomped in the stables. Her candle was burning low in the wall.

Some tiny animal scuttered across the floor with the faintest of sounds. Annie drew her feet up and clasped her hands around her knees. Rattlesnakes, flash floods, and the other hazards of the open road she could face; but not mice! Definitely, not mice.

A tiny breeze flickered the flame of the candle. Outside, the stars were still bright in the night sky. But Annie knew that dawn was close. Suddenly she made up her mind. They would not wait for Jim Castle to send word to Uncle

Luke that they were here. They would leave for Diablo before Jim Castle was awake. She must meet Uncle Luke without letting him know that she and Tagg had arrived. She wanted to surprise him, catch him off guard. It would give her a better chance of finding out what sort of a man he really was, and what kind of a home she was bringing Tagg into. The superintendent had seemed honest and sincere, and she hoped desperately that what he had said about politics in Diablo was the answer. But it was her responsibility to make sure—before she and Tagg were committed to staying.

She stepped down from the bed gingerly, with a cautious eye for the long-gone mouse. The sky outside was starting to turn gray. She must wake Tagg quietly, poor lamb, and they must be on their way before Jim Castle woke and tried to argue her out of it.

Long fingers of dawn were reaching across the sky to the east as Annie and Tagg tiptoed out of the headquarters building with their carpetbags and Annie's saddle. Annie had left the payment for their rooms on the counter in an envelope addressed to Jim Castle, with a short note telling him that she had decided not to bother her uncle by bringing him all the way from Diablo to meet her and Tagg.

A surprised and sleepy stable hand helped them harness up and, for an extra dime, opened the station gate for them. Annie rode out first on Target, and Tagg brought up the rear with the wagon. She hoped uneasily that the rumble of the wheels and the squeak of the ungreased axles would not arouse Jim Castle and bring him out, too. Her mind was made up, she was doing what she thought was best for Tagg and herself, and arguing about it would do no good.

She sighed with relief as the heavy gate closed behind them and she heard the iron bar drop back into place. So far, so good.

The air was still filled with the coolness of the night, but Annie knew that the moment the sun rose, it would be uncomfortably warm. There was a long road ahead through the rocky, treeless wasteland, and it was too much to hope that there would be a desert spring with its welcome greenness along the way. So, while traveling was still pleasant and easy, she set a rapid pace with Target, and they rolled merrily along.

It was less than an hour later that Annie, riding along at the side of the still briskly rolling wagon, thought she saw a wisp of smoke up ahead among the giant boulders that lined the narrow road. One moment it was there—

the next it was gone from sight.

She squinted her eyes and shielded them from the level rays of the rising sun. There was no more smoke. In fact, she reflected, it might not have been smoke at all, but a tiny whirlwind of sand blown unusually high. She threw a quick glance at Tagg. He hadn't seen it. If it *had* been smoke, it was probably a prospector's campfire, and there was nothing to get alarmed about. Those road agents were miles away by now.

She called over to Tagg, "If this map of Uncle Luke's is anywhere near right, we'll be at Diablo some time this afternoon."

"Maybe we'll spend tonight on Uncle Luke's ranch!" Tagg was gleeful. "And I'll meet my new pony!"

She nodded. "Better be thinking up a name for him as we go along," she suggested cheerfully.

That would keep his mind busy with something besides the possible dangers of the road ahead. But she was keeping her own rifle close at hand in the saddle scabbard, and her Colt hung loaded and ready at her side.

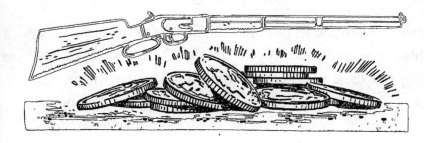

## 4        Twin Troublemakers

Annie had been right about that small puff of smoke she
thought she saw coming up from among the big rocks
that bordered the road ahead. It had drifted up from a cooking fire that was burning briskly under a battered frying
pan. A rough-looking man was hunkered down over
the fire, stirring a greasy, scorched mixture of bacon and
beans in the pan. A second man lay snoring a few feet away,
rolled in a blanket. Two horses stood in the early morning
shade of the big rocks and munched on dry tufts of grass.
Their saddles lay close by in an untidy heap.

The man at the fire turned a dirty, black-bearded face
to snarl at the sleeper. "Come on! Come on, roll out! It's
past sunup!"

The second man yawned widely and sat up. It was like
looking at two copies of the same picture to see a bearded

face just as black and dirty as the first, with the same beady black eyes and weak-lipped mouth. There was no mistaking that these two were not only brothers, but twins. The second man scratched his ribs sleepily, ran his fingers through the shock of greasy black hair that hung down unevenly over his forehead, and moved over to the fire.

"What's the hurry?" he protested. "I was just sleepin' good."

"We gotta hightail it back to Diablo and check in with the boss." His brother had helped himself to the contents of the frying pan, and spoke through a large mouthful of beans. "Maybe he's got another job for us, somethin' bigger this time."

"Okay, okay! But a man needs sleep. He ain't right unless he gits plenty of it."

"You sleep seven-eighths of the time and you still ain't right," snorted the other.

It was an old argument, carried on half-heartedly. Rufe and Rube Horton were really so much alike that neither actually found anything wrong about his twin. They just had to snarl at each other from time to time when there was no one else around to bully.

"Wait'll the boss hears you rid off with a case of eau-dee-cologney water, thinkin' it was somethin' worthwhile!"

His twin grunted. Then—"Anyhow, we got a coupla good watches in the haul, and more'n three hundred in greenbacks off them stage passengers." He sighed. "Wish we could keep it ourselves."

"Well, we can't. So eat up an' let's break camp an' head back."

They made short work of the scanty breakfast, and then Rufe lumbered to his feet and shuffled over toward the horses.

"Don't take all day saddlin' up." Rube was dumping the remains of the dirty dishes. "It's started to turn hot already."

"Quit orderin' me around." Rufe turned his head to bark back at his brother, and failed to notice one of the discarded blanket hoods lying on the ground in front of him. His feet tangled in it and he started to fall forward. He saved himself by clutching the mane of the nearest horse. It happened to be his own much-abused animal. The poor creature had taken many a beating from the uneven-tempered badman, and this seemed like the start of another. He snorted in fright and reared, pawing the air wildly.

Rufe swore angrily and jerked hard on the rope, half

checking the horse as he tried to subdue him. The animal's foot came down on a loose stone that rolled beneath it and threw him off balance. In a frantic struggle to keep his footing, the horse gashed his right foreleg on a jagged rock. The pain of the injury threw him into complete panic, and it took the combined efforts of the brothers to bring him under control. When he finally stood, shaking and quivering, they could see that the gash, while it looked bad, was not deep. He would be lame for a few days, and not much use for the kind of riding they usually had to do.

"Blasted hard luck critter, I oughta finish him off right now!" Rufe clapped his hand to the butt of his heavy six-shooter.

"Forget it!" his brother said sharply. "He'll be as good as new in a coupla days. Meantime, you better not try to ride him. We'll wrap up that leg and get him to the horse doc at Diablo."

"Yeah? Well, I ain't walkin' to oblige no mangy old cayuse."

"You don't have to walk. My Bucko'll carry double!"

"You know blame well he'll bog down in half a mile. An' if you think you can talk me—" he broke off suddenly to listen. "Wagon wheels!"

"Comin' from Smoke Tree," Rube decided. "Might be the stage highballin' back to Diablo off-schedule, on account of some big bad bandits holdin' it up last night."

"Yeah," Rufe nodded with a snaggle-toothed grin. "Maybe we oughta speed 'em on their way." He slapped the walnut handles of his tied-down six-shooters suggestively.

"Wait!" Rube listened with a scowl. "Wheels are squeakin'. Can't be the stage. I better take a look."

He checked his six-shooters quickly, then cautiously made his way between the boulders, keeping out of sight of the oncoming wagon.

Now he could see what it was. His mouth twisted in a contemptuous sneer. Just a girl on a horse, and a kid driving a rickety old farm wagon loaded with furniture. Pilgrims. Probably didn't have a dollar between them. It would be a waste of time to try to rob them. He was moving back when he realized that Rufe had come up behind him and was staring past him at the pair.

"Nothin' to bother about there," Rube whispered. "Jist shoe-stringers."

But Rufe held his ground. He nodded toward the girl on the horse. "That's a likely lookin' cow pony," he said.

"Mebbe I could trade her my old crowbait for him."

Rube took another look. "What are we waitin' for? Take 'im!"

"Reckon I will, at that!"

The warm still air was stirring a little now, and the smell of a wood fire came faintly to Annie's nose, mingled with the aroma of fried bacon. She was not really conscious of what it was. It just made her vaguely hungry, and reminded her suddenly that she had rushed Tagg away from the station without breakfast. The poor lamb!

She reined in and waited for the wagon to catch up with her. Tagg was sniffing the air.

"I smell bacon!" he announced. "Boy!"

"I thought I did, too," she admitted. She looked keenly about, but there was no sign of a campfire or a friendly prospector anywhere. "Guess it was just imagination and an empty tummy. We'd better stop right here and cure it!"

Tagg was more than willing. He sawed on the reins and brought the mules to a stop.

Annie swung off Target and dropped the reins across his neck, letting them trail on the ground. She knew that he would stay there until she came back to him or called him to her. He nosed the sandy ground for a possible tuft of grass, but he didn't find anything promising, so he lowered his head and closed his eyes for a nap.

Annie looked around for a good place to start the cooking fire. There was plenty of kindling in the wagon, now, thanks to the obliging stableman who had helped them on their way. She took an armful of short sticks and knelt to build up her fire in the shelter of a small rock. She went about it expertly, and with no suspicion that two pairs of beady black eyes were watching every move.

Tagg yawned and stretched as he jumped down off the wagon seat and went around behind the wagon to get out the breakfast things.

Annie was bending to blow the sparks of her fire into flame. Her back was turned to Target, but she heard him snort, and she knew from the kind of sound he made that something was frightening him. Swift as a cat, she was on her feet in an instant, had swung around, and leveled her Colt at the gray-hooded man who had a grip on Target's reins and was trying to drag the cow pony away with him. Target was braced against the pull, snorting and digging in with his four feet.

"Let go!" she called out, "or I'll shoot!"

"Don't talk foolish, miss!" The thick-sounding voice came from over at the wagon. "Put away that gun before it goes off an' hurts yuh! We know you're bluffin'!"

Annie wheeled at the first word. A second gray-hooded man had caught Tagg from behind and was using him as a shield. His left arm was tight across Tagg's throat, and the boy's feet were off the ground. He was gasping for breath, feebly tearing at the arm that was choking him. The hooded man held a six-shooter lightly in his other hand and gestured carelessly with it as he spoke.

She thought fast. If she shot now, and smashed the man's gun, the flying metal might cut Tagg badly. She cast a quick glance over her shoulder toward Target. The gallant little pony was more than holding his own against the cursing man. Annie lowered her Colt, and slipped it into the holster.

"That's more like it!" The man who was holding Tagg let him drop. Tagg fell limply and rolled over, clutching his throat and gasping. The man flourished his gun. "Now, just do like we tell yuh—"

Annie's Colt flashed lightning-swift from its holster again, and she aimed and fired in one motion. The long six-shooter leaped out of the hooded man's hand and flew

through the air in a hundred pieces. He yelped in pain
and nursed his hand. Tagg scrambled away and Annie
wheeled on the man who was trying to subdue Target.
Her quick shot clipped off the high heel of his boot. Thrown
off balance, he toppled over backward and fell heavily.
When he rolled over and tried to make a fast draw, Annie's
third shot plowed into the sand six inches from his other
boot. "Don't try it," she called. "Get your hands up!"

He glared at her through the eye-holes of the hood, but
his hands went up—high. "Keep them that way," she
advised, gesturing with the Colt, "and stay where you are."

"Look out, Annie!" It was Tagg's yell. Annie whirled
to see the other hooded man making a fast left-handed
draw. Her bullet hit his revolver before it was out of his
holster, and there was a deafening roar of a double explo-
sion. She was ready for another shot, but Rube Horton had
had enough. He dropped the smoking remains of his
second gun and ran out of sight among the boulders. Annie
turned toward the man on the ground, her gun still ready,
but he was not looking for more trouble. He sat up with
his hands over his head.

"Pull off that hood!" she ordered. Rufe Horton hesitated only a second, then he slowly obeyed.

Annie and Tagg stared at the dirty, black-bearded face with its small, shiny, black, animal eyes. His lips were drawn back in a defiant snarl, but he eyed the six-shooter in her hand with respect.

"We didn't figger to do you any hurt, miss. We jist wanted the hoss," he whined.

Over among the boulders, Rube Horton was riding out, leading his twin's lame horse after him. Rufe turned to scowl after him. He muttered angrily under his breath. Even at that distance, Annie could see the rough bandage on the led horse's foreleg, and she guessed why the men had tried to steal Target.

She knew, from the evidence of the gray hoods, that these were the men who had held up the stage last night. As she watched Rube disappear among the sand hills to the north, she was quite sure she would have no more trouble with him before she got to Diablo. And she made up her mind what she was going to do with this one. She was going to take him along and see what the law would do to him.

She motioned him to get on his feet. The missing boot heel gave him a list to one side, like a man climbing around the side of a hill.

"How far is it to Diablo from here?" Annie asked him.

Rufe hesitated. This sunny-haired girl might be a good shot and one of the fastest draws he had ever met—but she was still only a woman. He decided to try for sympathy. "Eight miles, ma'am," he whined. "A powerful long way in the hot sun. I hope you ain't fixin' to make me walk."

Annie winked at Tagg who grinned back at her. "What do you say, Tagg? It might slow us down a bit."

"Sure would, Annie."

"All right, then, we'll let him ride. Bring the lasso rope and we'll take Uncle Luke a new boarder for his jail."

She had brought in her uncle's name deliberately, to see what effect it would have on the prisoner. She hoped he would look worried. Instead, he yawned and let them tie him up and bundle him into the wagon, without comment.

Later, after Tagg had eaten all the breakfast he wanted, and they were ready to start for Diablo, Annie tried again.

"We'll take along that hood," she told Tagg, tucking it into the wagon beside the prisoner. "Uncle Luke will want to use it as evidence about last night."

This time, she saw a mocking look in the small animal eyes, and a sneering smile twisting his lips. It was plain that the Diablo sheriff and his jail held no terrors for this particular road agent. For some reason, he was not worried.

Annie was disturbed. She tried to dismiss the sneer from her mind as she set the wagon in motion and mounted Target for the last lap of their journey.

But it didn't stay away. It came back during the rest of the long hot ride to Diablo and tormented her with doubts. Why wasn't this holdup man and horse thief afraid of her uncle's authority? Had that loud-talking salesman been right last night when he said that Luke MacTavish closed his eyes to crime in his county?

She would soon be in a position to find out.

It seemed an endless ride to Annie, but at last she sighted the town she had traveled so far to reach. It was like twenty others they had passed through in the last four weeks since they had left the greener valleys of the eastern end of the trail. The life of the town flowed lazily through one dusty main street. Weathered frame buildings lined the street, and—except for the freshly painted land office—all had been there many years. Cow horses stood at the hitch-racks, and booted, spurred men of the saddle trod the warped boards of the sidewalks. Down at one end of the street, the sheriff's adobe office and jail stood apart.

As Annie led the way through the dusty street toward
the jail, the black-bearded prisoner in her wagon leaned
forward and stared at the gold-lettered window of the neat
land office—*John Shanley, Land and Mining Agent,* the
shiny letters read.

A face appeared suddenly at the window—Rube Horton's
face. The prisoner's eyes met his, and Rube made a quick
sign of reassurance before he disappeared again into the
shadows of the office. In the wagon, Rufe gave a contented
sigh and settled back. Everything was under control. The
wagon creaked on its way.

In the land office, the fashionably dressed, handsome,
middle-aged man behind the big roll-top desk looked at
Rube Horton disgustedly.

"You and your precious brother are more trouble than
you're worth, Horton! I told you to make that stage holdup last night a quick job, and then duck. By now, you
should be miles away. Instead, you ride in here, leave those
two crowbait nags of yours in my alley for anybody who
was on that stage to recognize—and that brother of yours
gets himself tied up by a greenhorn girl and a little boy!"

Rube scowled. "Nobody'll know our horses. And if you

ever saw that settler gal out there handle a six-gun, you wouldn't be so uppity about her!"

"Oh, get out of here!" Wealthy John Shanley pulled half a dozen coins from his well-filled purse and scattered them across the desk at Rube. "Here's your pay—in good Denver coin. Now get out of town and stay out till I send for you again."

"What happens to Rufe?" The black-bearded twin was hungrily gathering up the gold coins. "They got him dead to rights on that horse-stealin'."

"I'll look after him." John Shanley waved him away. "Now go, and don't try any more jobs that I don't order. I'll let you know when I need you again."

Shanley watched Rube Horton leave by the back door. Then he locked it securely and went back to his high-topped desk. He settled in the deep leather chair and selected a slender Havana cigar from his silver-trimmed humidor. Those cigars cost him almost as much as the food for his whole stylish establishment at the other end of town, he reflected, but they were well worth it. They were his trademark. He was the only man in town who could afford such extravagance, and it stamped him as a leader. He had clinched many a sale of a mining claim or a doubtful lot far out on the desert, with a gift of one of those expensive cigars!

He smiled at his own shrewdness, but the smile disappeared as he took out a map of Diablo that he kept locked in the small drawer labeled *Private*. Each lot on the main street was marked, some initialed J. S., others with different initials. He studied the map with a frown. There were still too many other initials on business lots that he wanted, but there was no doubt in his mind that he would change that before too long.

The thing that made him frown was the string of neatly plotted lots that extended from the north edge of town out toward the hills. They were all marked with size and number—a number that corresponded with certain records in his ledger. They were all sold, those lots—sold to people who had never seen them—*yet*. That was the rub. He had sold them by advertisement in the big Boston papers, to people who believed what they read, and who wanted to make their homes in the rich new country they had heard so much about, where gold and silver were lying in the streets to be picked up by anyone. And with the coming of fall, most of those eager buyers would be coming to claim the land they had bought. John Shanley had to be ready to deliver legal title to it. The only thing that stood in the way of this happy ending was that Shanley had sold many thousands of dollars' worth of property that he had no right to sell. It belonged to someone else.

Across the map, just a short distance beyond the edge of the town itself, ran a firm black line that cut through the neatly drawn and numbered lots. It was a boundary line—the southern boundary of a ranch. It wasn't a very large ranch, as ranches go, only a hundred and sixty acres —practically no land at all in that country of great distances, but it stood in John Shanley's way. And it was a threat to him and the rich future he planned. Because, if John Shanley could not wipe out those boundaries before his customers came flocking out to claim their land, he might end up in jail, not only disgraced and branded a crook, but cheated out of his political ambitions forever. A man who hoped to be governor some day, when the Territory gained its statehood, had to have a clean record.

He was not especially worried at the moment. He had made a fair offer to the owner of the little ranch. True, it had been refused, much to Shanley's surprise and annoyance. He had had no idea he would be delayed by a refusal. He had offered a larger price than the land was worth, just to make sure there would be no delay. And then the stubborn old fool said, "No, I've decided not to sell. I've got other plans." And he had stuck with that decision and been strangely mysterious about those plans. "Can't sell to anybody now," he had chuckled. "I need that ranch."

Shanley had tried several times to change his mind, but the answer was always no. So Shanley had made other plans. And he had been going ahead with them very successfully so far. When he was finished with stubborn old Luke Mac-Tavish, there would be a new sheriff in Diablo, and Luke would be in such disgrace that he would be glad to sell out and leave the town forever.

Shanley's campaign was costing him a lot of gold pieces, but it was worth it, with his whole future hanging in the balance. At first he had felt a touch of regret. Luke had been a good friend. And no one knew better than Shanley that the sheriff was honest and trustworthy. But John Shanley had to have that ranch, and quickly. That was all that mattered now.

Up at the end of the street, in front of the jail, Annie dismounted and looped Target's reins around the hitch-rail. Tagg brought up the wagon, and Annie tied the mules before she went around to get the prisoner.

A group of men had gathered quietly to watch. Annie's eyes swept them quickly. They seemed to be only mildly interested. They stared, but no one asked any questions, and no one offered to give her a hand with the prisoner. She helped him out of the wagon and he stood lopsidedly waiting. She had a curious feeling that these citizens of Diablo were taking a "hands off" attitude.

A bold-looking man in a Stetson was nearest. She asked him, "Is the sheriff in? I have a prisoner for him."

"Now, that's real obliging of you, miss," he answered loudly. Annie could tell it was meant for the crowd to hear. "He shore don't bring in any himself these days."

"What d'ya expect?" came a taunting voice from the edge of the crowd.

Annie's eyes flashed in that direction, but she couldn't distinguish the speaker. There were several men snickering, and there were several others who were scowling. She felt the same uneasiness that had kept her awake all night. Something was wrong when people laughed like that at hearing their sheriff belittled.

She nudged the prisoner ahead of her toward the sheriff's office. The door was standing open. She would soon know what kind of a man her mother's brother had become.

## 5         Countercharges

Inside the small jail, a gray-haired man with a lined, weather-beaten face sat frowning unhappily at the official-looking letter he had spread out on the pine table he used for a desk. He wore the five-pointed star that identified him as sheriff of Diablo County, and his Frontier Colt hung from the gun belt slung over the back of his chair. Luke MacTavish was having a bad time.

It wasn't the first time Sheriff Luke had had a letter that bore the Territorial seal and was signed with the governor's own sprawling signature. In the past few months he had had several of them, but this was the strongest.

*Either take steps to clean the outlaws out of your district,* it warned, in effect, *or it will be necessary to ask for your resignation as sheriff of Diablo County at once. There have been several charges made that no effort is being made to*

*put an end to the violence and crime around Diablo. A
check of the records shows that few arrests have been made,
and the district is rapidly getting a lawless reputation.*

The letter was written in the usual official secretarial
handwriting, with its Spencerian flourishes; but across the
bottom, in his old friend the governor's familiar hen-tracks,
he read: *For your own sake as well as mine, Luke, do something quick about this! You know I'm for you a hundred
per cent, but with the elections so near, I'm under pressure.
I can't let things get out of hand in any part of the Territory.
I'm counting on you to round up those lawbreakers even if
you have to deputize every man in Diablo County to do it.
Get busy!*

                                    *Your old friend, Stubby.*

It was easy enough to write, "round them up," when
you were sitting in a soft leather chair in the governor's
mansion up at the capital, but it was another thing to be
able to go out and do it. How do you round up shadows?

Luke MacTavish had done his best, but while he was
out with his only deputy trying to track down the men who
had just robbed a bank, a stagecoach would be held up,
and its passengers robbed, a few miles away. Sometimes the
gray-masked outlaws worked as a pair, other times one man

struck swiftly and rode away alone. Occasionally there
would be three of them. They worked by day and by night.
And a growing number of victims were getting louder in
their criticism, as Sheriff Luke and his deputy constantly
failed to bring in the criminals who were making him look
clumsy and inefficient. And now his old friend the governor had begun to feel the political effects of the situation.
It couldn't go on much longer.

The worst part of it was the way people who had always
been his friends and supporters were turning against him
in his own town. He knew what they were whispering in
Diablo; that he was getting too old to be depended on to
keep law and order there any more—that it was time he
stepped aside for a younger, more active man who could
run the lawbreakers back into the hills and make the
county safe for new settlers, and old as well.

He looked up startled as Annie herded the scowling
Rufe Horton ahead of her through the doorway. Rufe's
hands were lifted shoulder-high, and he was walking with
an odd swinging gait because of the missing boot heel.

Annie's wide-brimmed hat was pushed back off her
pretty face, and her blue eyes were stern as she held the
heavy army revolver leveled at the badman's back.

Luke rose quickly and came around the table.

"Well, what's this?" he inquired.

"Sheriff MacTavish?" Annie's tone was business-like.

"That's right, little lady." The sheriff's smile was a bit puzzled. "What have you rounded up here?"

"This feller tried to steal my horse a few miles back on the road from Smoke Tree Station. I had to shoot his boot heel off, but he isn't hurt."

MacTavish scowled at Rufe Horton. "What do you say for yourself, mister?"

The badman met his eye with a defiant scowl. "Nothin'," he sneered, "to *you!* I'll do my talkin' in front of a judge, where everybody can hear me." He looked scornfully at Annie and then turned back to Luke. "That is, if you two think you can put this over on anybody."

Annie had been studying the kindly, weather-beaten face of her uncle as he and the outlaw came face to face. She had been afraid that she would see some sign of recognition or guilt on his face. Instead, she had read only surprise, and now, quick anger at the sneering badman's words. She felt relieved and happy.

"What are you talking about? This young lady claims you tried to steal her horse, and I'm aimin' to hold you on that charge. That's all there is to it."

"Maybe it is, an' maybe it ain't!" Rufe swaggered and smirked knowingly. "We'll see."

Sheriff Luke turned to Annie with a puzzled expression. "Do you have any idea what he's driving at, miss?"

Her eyes flashed angrily. "Sounds like some kind of a bluff to me, Sheriff, but he's forgetting something."

She brought up her left hand with the gray hood that he had worn when he tried to steal Target. "He—and the man who was with him—both were wearing hoods when he tried to take my horse. The other feller rode off, still wearing one. And this is *his*."

Sheriff Luke snatched it from her hand. His eyes were snapping with excitement. "Gray blanket hood—holes cut in for eyes—" he checked. "This is great, miss!" He flashed a wide grin at her that reminded her strongly of Tagg. "Looks to me like you've caught quite a fish, young lady. We've been after these gray-hooded road agents for a long spell, and this is the first time we've caught up with one of them. I'm sure much obliged to you." He turned on Rufe. "Reckon you'll be boarding here for a considerable spell, Mr. Horse Thief."

Annie smiled. "I think you'll find he was mixed up in

that stagecoach robbery last night along the Smoke Tree road, as well. The two men who did it wore hoods like this, I heard."

Sheriff Luke nodded. "Wouldn't be a mite surprised! We'll hold him on attempted horse-stealing and add the rest later on, if the driver can tie him up with it."

"You better change your mind about holding me on such a faked-up yarn." The contemptuous tone in the black-bearded prisoner's voice startled Annie. "You two just try bringin' me to trial, and I'll git the laugh on you."

"I happen to have a witness," Annie flashed. The man's self-assurance worried her. She could see that it was bothering the sheriff, too.

"Oh, sure! You've got your kid brother. *That'll* help—I don't think!" Rufe laughed loudly.

MacTavish's lined face was red with anger as he towered over the sneering badman. "You won't be laughing when the jury gets through with you! This town's fed up with being pestered by your kind of varmint, and I aim to see they make an example out of you!"

"You don't say!" Rufe sneered. "Why, the whole county'll be laughing at the old has-been that ain't had the nerve for years to make a real arrest! Wait'll the word gits around that you an' her cooked up a fake charge so you could claim to be on the job! They'll hoot yuh outa town!"

The sheriff glared at him. "Why, I never saw this young woman before in my life!" He turned to Annie. "Did I, miss?"

"Hey, Annie!" The voice came from the direction of the front door. They all looked over quickly. It was Tagg, grinning at her and the tall man. "Is this Uncle Luke?"

"Uncle—?" Sheriff MacTavish looked from the boy to Annie. She smiled and nodded.

"I'm Tagg!" Tagg came up with his hand held out. The tall sheriff took it automatically, and Tagg shook his hand briskly. "And she's Annie! We just got here."

"So I see!" Luke was still a little bewildered by the disclosure.

Rufe Horton watched with a sneering smile, as Luke turned to Annie. "Why didn't you say who you were right off, child?"

"I thought it was just as well to wait till you had this varmint locked up."

"We'll tend to that right now." Luke reached for the cell key on his desk. "Come on, mister."

"Better change your mind about it," the black-bearded

one stood his ground. "It ain't gonna sound good in court."

"What's he talking about, Annie?" Tagg scowled at the badman.

"He's trying to wiggle out of the horse-stealing charge by saying that Uncle Luke and I cooked it up together." She smiled cheerfully at the badman. "But it won't work. He can't fool anybody with such a silly story."

"Yeah?" Rufe Horton glared at her. "We'll see who gits fooled before we're through."

"That's enough big talk!" Sheriff Luke gripped his arm and led him toward the cells.

Out in the alley behind the jail, Rube Horton rode by slowly, leading Rufe's lame horse behind him. He studied the two small high cell windows with their heavy bars. They were above a man's height, but he could reach them easily by using the cracks in the old adobe wall as a foothold. He would be back later.

He rode on, unnoticed, and soon was out of town and on his way up into the hills. He was headed toward a small, one-room shack they had used from time to time. He would wait there till dark, and then mosey back down to Diablo to talk to his brother through the cell windows. He was not sure that John Shanley would get Rufe out of jail as easily as he thought. The Hortons took wages from the land agent, but they never trusted anyone very far—except each other.

In the jail, Rufe was enjoying a meal of fried chicken and dumplings. It was much tastier food than he and Rube were used to, and he wolfed it down with much gusto. Between bites, he reflected that maybe they had been missing a bet by not letting themselves be arrested now and then, if jail food was this good!

If Rufe had only known it, he wasn't eating regular jail food. That particular chicken dinner had been cooked for tall, good-looking Deputy Lofty Craig, by a love-smitten young waitress at the hotel. She had gone to a lot of pains to see that it was done just the way Lofty had told her he liked it, and had brought it over to the jail herself to give it to the shy young man. But, alas, Lofty had been out on an errand, and the sheriff had accepted it for him, with many thanks.

The sheriff had promptly handed it over to his prisoner with a sigh of relief that for one night, at least, he wouldn't have to cook a meal for his captive. Cooking was one of the duties that went with the sheriff's job, and Sheriff Luke could never seem to cook anything without scorching it.

As Lofty had confided to the pretty waitress only that morning, in a bid for a free meal, "One of these days somebody's due to figure out how to burn water, and Luke'll be the first to learn!"

By the time Lofty came on duty, the only trace of that dinner was a small pile of chicken bones. Sheriff Luke kept a discreet silence as he saw his deputy casting hopeful looks in the direction of the hotel. He knew Lofty would find out all about the purloined dinner, next time he met the pretty girl.

Annie carefully sized up the tall young deputy as she met him. His clothes were worn, and his boots were old. If *he* was the one whose actions were bringing criticism on the sheriff's office, he certainly showed no signs of enjoying any of the loot. She decided she would keep an eye on him and watch for signs; but for now she wouldn't say anything about her suspicions to Uncle Luke. He seemed to have enough to worry about.

With the prisoner safely locked up, and Lofty on guard till morning, Sheriff Luke was as excited as Tagg as he prepared to take them out to the ranch.

"Maybe the place'll seem small to you," he told Annie, "but it's been home to me ever since your mother and I came out to settle twenty-five years ago with your grandpa, and fought Indians all the way from Iowa. Your grandpa's buried out there; and your dad and mother were married in our parlor. The old ranch is only a hop, skip, and a jump from town now, and the town's getting closer all the time; but it was a long way from civilization back in those days. I recollect feeling right sad when I saw that Sis—your mother—was showin' signs of fallin' in love with that good-lookin' young cavalry officer from the fort, but I didn't let on for fear she'd get to thinkin' it was her duty to stay single and keep house for me." He smiled at his memories. "She was a mighty sweet bride, if I do say it myself, an' I know she was right happy with you young'uns and your dad, till the fever took her off, but I've never got over missin' her around the place."

Annie nodded, and her eyes were misty with unshed tears. "I can imagine," she told him softly, "she and Dad were both pretty special." She glanced at Tagg who was hanging over Deputy Lofty's shoulder, watching him clean his new Winchester rifle. "I only wish the young feller there had had a chance to grow up knowing them. But what little he saw of Dad he won't forget, and I know you'll have lots to tell him about them both."

"You bet I will." Sheriff Luke smiled warmly at his niece. "And we're going to be mighty happy out there, just us three, for a long, long time!"

Tagg watched every move as Deputy Lofty cleaned and then deftly reassembled the Winchester. It was the first time Tagg had been that close to one of the late model repeating rifles, and he was still awed by the fact that it fired five shots without reloading. "Golly whiz!" he exclaimed. "What Annie could do with that!"

Lofty looked surprised, and a little amused. "This," he told Tagg, patting the shiny weapon, "is strictly a man's gun. It would be mighty dangerous if a person didn't know how to handle it. But one of these days I may let her try, if she thinks she could learn."

Tagg choked back a giggle, and kept his face straight.

They were ready to leave for the ranch now. Sheriff Luke tucked the governor's letter into an inner pocket of his worn jacket. He was still deeply troubled, but he meant to forget everything for a while, except getting his little family comfortably settled. That was the most important thing. His family. It gave him a warm glow just to say it over to himself. He hadn't realized how lonely he had been these past years.

Up the street, John Shanley locked up his land office. He hald sold a couple of rather doubtful claims today, but it was all perfectly legitimate. He had tucked a couple of extra Havana cigars in his breast pocket to give his old friend Sheriff Luke as he stopped by the jail. He planned to be impressed by the capture of the badman. Then he would suggest, very casually of course, that perhaps the settler girl had been mistaken, and the prisoner had really intended to *buy* her horse, not steal it. He would speak of how hysterical a woman could get over a thing like that. He hoped that Rufe Horton would hear and have brains enough to follow that line in his own defense. He was pretty sure that if Luke thought there had been a mistake, he would let Rufe off with a warning.

"Stupid old fool," he thought, contemptuously. "Well, he'll soon be out of my way!"

## 6             Getting Acquainted

"Up you go, boy!" Sheriff Luke lifted Tagg over the wheel of the wagon and into the driver's seat. Annie watched and smiled to herself, as she swung into her saddle. Tagg, who hated anybody to help him, was actually saying thanks to their new-found uncle for the lift! It looked as if the family was going to get along famously.

Annie swung Target around, and narrowly missed bumping the tall, dignified man in the black coat and stovepipe hat. He dodged nimbly aside with an expression of annoyance and anger. "Be careful, young woman!" he snapped, shaking his gold-headed cane at her.

"Sorry, mister." Annie leaned down with her most polite smile. "I didn't notice you were so close."

Sheriff Luke turned quickly at the sound of their voices, and hurried over, beaming. "John!" he exclaimed, "you're just in time. I want you to meet my niece and nephew, Annie and Tagg Oakley. They've come to live with me! This is Mr. Shanley, Annie, one of my very best friends, and, to my way of thinking, Diablo's leading citizen!"

John Shanley tried to hold a pleased smile on his face as he acknowledged the introductions. It was a painful effort. So this was why the stubborn old goat had refused to sell his miserable ranch!

It was an unexpected setback for Shanley. Now, no matter how inefficient, or even dishonest, the sheriff was made to seem to the people of Diablo, he would fight to hold his job, because he would want to make a home for these two. And even though he lost the job, he would want to hold on to the ranch while Annie and her brother were here!

Sheriff Luke was babbling on happily, and Shanley forced himself to agree that it *was* a fine surprise and he *was* most happy for his old friend Luke.

"Uncle Luke was just telling me," Annie smiled at Shanley, "that he almost sold you the ranch a few months ago. Wasn't it lucky he didn't? We wouldn't have had any place to live!"

"Yes, indeed!" John Shanley's voice sounded hollow to himself, but he hoped no one else noticed it. "Well, if he *had* sold it to me," he reassured her, "I'd have been happy to sign it right back to him when he found out he needed it!"

"Of course you would have!" Sheriff Luke clapped his old friend heartily on the back. "But right the very day I had my mind made up to sell, I got Annie's letter tellin' me about her dad bein' killed by the Injuns, and them havin' no place to stay now, so I changed my mind quick."

"Didn't you tell Mr. Shanley why?" Annie was surprised.

"Nope!" Sheriff Luke grinned again with the same look she had so often seen on Tagg's mischievous little face. "I thought I'd keep it to myself, so if you two decided not to come here, I could stand it better without havin' folks sympathizin'."

Shanley made himself laugh heartily with the sheriff, and he was loud in his admiration as Luke told him how Annie had captured a gray-hooded would-be horse thief. "Good for you, little lady!" he beamed. "And, Luke, maybe it'll change your luck, now you've caught one of those troublemakers."

"The point is," the big sheriff sighed, "I didn't even catch *this* one. Annie did!"

"All in the family, Luke!" Shanley waved it aside genially. "And speaking of family," he smiled up at Annie, "I have a girl just about your age. She'll be home in a day or two for the summer, from boarding school. I'm counting on you two getting to be great friends."

"Why, thanks, Mr. Shanley," Annie beamed. "I'd be most happy to know her, and I hope she'll like me."

A few minutes later, John Shanley watched the sheriff and Annie ride out ahead of the lumbering mule-drawn wagon with Tagg sitting up straight on the seat and flourishing his whip in great style. There was no friendly warmth in Shanley's eyes now, only cold dislike that took in the girl and boy, as well as his former friend. He must get a telegram off to Edith at once. He rather dreaded the rumpus it would cause. His daughter was up at the capital, spending her school vacation with friends. He knew she would be furious when he ordered her home to Diablo. She hated the town, and most of its people, but she would come when he told her to. She knew better than to disobey orders. Of course, he might have to bribe her to stay, with an extra allowance for school next term. Or he might promise to let her go abroad with some of her classmates next winter. Whatever it cost, he had to have her here now.

So the telegram was sent, and afterward Shanley rode up toward the hide-out camp where his twin badmen usually "holed up" between their activities for him. He rode only half the distance, because Rube had already started back down to have a talk through the jail window with his twin. Shanley and the black-bearded Rube talked briefly, and then the land agent turned his horse and rode home to his imposing house on the edge of town.

The badman went back up to the cabin to saddle a second horse, and wait for darkness before he started out again to carry out Shanley's orders.

John Shanley rode through the tall gates in the spiked iron fence that set his mansion off from the rest of Diablo. He had sent to Pittsburgh for that impressive fencing. Only one other house in Diablo had anything like it—Ben Crane's. The owner of the Lucy K. mine had copied Shanley, but Crane's fence wasn't within a foot so tall, or the iron gates half so ornate. And Crane's house didn't have the fancy scrollwork all along the upper edge of the veranda, nor the handsome cupola rising a full story above the rest of the house, to give it an air of proud distinction.

Why, even the lush green lawn and the flowers around

the mansion cost more each month to keep up than the common Diabloite spent in a year on food! Maybe next year, he mused, he would install a fountain, right in the middle of the lawn. *That* would be something in the forsaken desert country! They would talk about that all the way up to the capital! Then, one of these days—in the governor's mansion, he would—

He frowned in sudden recollection. There would be no fountain, not even a green-lawned mansion, unless he got his hands on that ranch of Luke MacTavish's before the people he had sold it to came to claim it!

Out at Sheriff MacTavish's snug little Bull's-Eye ranch, Annie and Tagg were just pulling in with their wagon. Luke had ridden ahead to open the heavy wooden gates that enclosed the tree-shaded yard.

Annie caught her breath as she stared at the weathered old ranch house, shaded by the big oak trees. The wide cool porch stretched the full width of the house, and morning-glory vines climbed up the square wooden pillars to the second story. It seemed to Annie as if she had seen it many times before. Her mother had described it so often, when she was small.

There was the well, near the house because, with the danger of Indian raids, it had to be. In case of a long siege, even though food supplies were to run short, folks could still live as long as they could get drinking water.

Luke could hardly wait to show them around. "Let the animals stand a few minutes," he called from the front porch. "I want you to see the place first by daylight."

Tagg hurried along by Annie's side, skipping in his excitement. Suddenly he stopped and pulled her by the sleeve. His eyes were round and troubled. "He hasn't said anything about my pony yet," he whispered. "D'ya think he forgot to buy it?"

Annie smiled and shook her head. "I doubt it, punkins. I don't think Uncle Luke's the kind who promises and then forgets. Just hold on."

"Come on, come on," the big man was holding open the front door for them. "As your grandpa used to say to all his visitors, 'Light an' come in, folks! The house is yours!'"

The last level rays of the desert sun were striking straight through the small west windows of the ranch house living room, bathing everything in the big quiet room with a golden glow. Annie stood in the doorway and looked slowly around. It all seemed so familiar to her. There was her grandfather's curio cabinet with curved glass doors. It was still filled with rock specimens, all neatly labeled and arranged. And over against the opposite wall—that must be "Papa's desk," a dark mahogany structure that reached almost to the eight-foot ceiling. It had come overland without a scratch, in a day when lesser pieces of furniture had met an untimely end in some swift river or on a steep mountain grade of the savage new land.

This was the home her mother had loved—the home she had left behind to travel from one far-off Army outpost to another with her young officer husband. Annie knew how she had missed it, but knew, too, that her mother had been happy with her little family, and wouldn't have changed places with anyone.

"Well, how do you like it?" Luke had been watching her hopefully.

Annie had to swallow a lump in her throat before she could answer. "Oh, Uncle Luke! It's just like Mother said it was!"

The weather-beaten face beamed. "I've kept her room just the way she left it, too. It's waitin' for you to move in."

Annie sighed contentedly. "It's good to be home," she said. And Tagg, tired out after the long day's excitement, yawned and nodded in sleepy agreement.

It was several hours later that Rube Horton came riding back down the trail to Diablo, and into the sleeping settlement by a side road. This time he led a saddled horse behind him. He dismounted quickly in the deserted alley back of the jail, and tied the two horses loosely to a post in an old shed.

He could see a faint flickering light inside the two high, barred windows in the adobe jail wall, as he moved cautiously through the shadows.

There was a wide enough crack in the old wall for him to gain a toe-hold and lift himself up on a level with the windows. He chose the nearest, and listened for a moment beneath it for voices. Everything was quiet inside. Cautiously, inch by inch, he drew himself up till he could see over the wide window sill. On a straw mattress less than ten feet away from the window, Rufe was stretched out on his bunk, asleep and snoring—as usual.

Rube's beady black eyes swept past his brother to the locked cell door, and beyond it to the main room of the jail. Lofty Craig was playing solitaire at the big pine table that the sheriff used for a desk. His back was to the cell, and he seemed to be keeping an eye on the closed front door. He had his gun belt off and lying on the table close to his right hand.

Rube scratched his finger lightly against the rough adobe window sill. Rufe stopped snoring at once. Rube scratched again—a tiny sound. Rufe's eyes opened and he stared up at the window. He caught a glimpse of his brother's face —then it disappeared.

After a moment, Rufe yawned loudly and scraped his feet on the floor, as he got noisily off the mattress and got up. He took a quick look and saw that Lofty was still busy with his card game. "Hey, deppity," he called, "you gonna keep that light shinin' in my face all night?"

The tall deputy threw the words over his shoulder at Rufe. "Turn your back if it bothers you."

"It's past my bedtime," the badman complained. "It ain't legal to keep me awake. It's cruelty, that's what!" He was stirring about, making as much noise as possible, and keeping an eye on Lofty's back. By now he was leaning carelessly against the wall beneath the high window. He squinted up and out at the sky. "Hey," he called back to Lofty, "I can see the Big Dipper." He held the bars and peered out.

Lofty grunted. He was annoyed at the interruptions.

"Take a drink out of it and quit pestering me."

Outside the window, Rube spoke in a quick, soft whisper to the man in the cell. Rufe shuffled his feet, and whistled "The Prisoner's Song" in a mournful key till his brother had finished giving him Shanley's orders. Then he reached up and made an okay sign with thumb and forefinger to the man outside the cell window.

Lofty was shuffling the cards for a new game when he heard a loud grunt and a sudden yowl of pain from Rufe. He dropped the cards and came to his feet, grabbing his gun belt from the table and wheeling to face Rufe's cell. By now, Rufe was moaning and groaning on the mattress. Lofty strode back to the cell door and stared through the bars at the black-bearded prisoner, now doubled up and giving vent to horrible groans of pain, as he clutched his mid-section.

"What ails *you*?" Lofty demanded suspiciously.

"I dunno," gasped the badman. "It hit me hard all of a sudden. Musta been that chicken I et."

"Chicken? What chicken?" Lofty was beginning to guess what had happened to the chicken dinner his waitress friend had promised him.

"That crummy stuff your boss give me for dinner," the

sufferer moaned. "Git me a doc, quick! I'm dyin'!" He rolled off the mattress to the cell floor, groaning horribly.

Lofty strapped on his gun belt before he went to the cell door and unlocked it. He kept his hand close to the butt of his six-shooter. If Horton was faking, he was ready. One sign of a trick, and the man writhing on the floor would find Lofty's gun in his ribs.

But Rufe continued to moan and clutch at his stomach, as Lofty leaned over him and shook him by the shoulder. He seemed sick enough, and the young deputy felt a little ashamed of his suspicions. He tried to lift the prisoner, but Rufe went limp. It took both Lofty's hands to drag him back toward the mattress. Rufe's feet scraped on the rough floor.

Lofty was too busy to hear the front door opening, or to notice the swift padding of stockinged feet behind him. He felt a sudden crashing blow on the back of his head. Then, for a long time—nothing.

7                                        Welcome Home

Out at the ranch, Annie was tucking Tagg into bed, in the
room that had been Luke MacTavish's when he was growing up. It was a snug little room, but Annie's nose wrinkled
at the dust that lay on everything except the clean sheets
that Luke had kept laid away for goodness knows how
long, waiting to be used. She thought about the houseclean-
ing she would start tomorrow. Why, some of this dust must
be older than Tagg himself! But that was a man's way of
housekeeping!

Tagg's sleepy eyes lingered on the various trophies hung
around the room. They must have been there, most of
them, since Luke was Tagg's own age. Here was an old
coyote skin, nailed to the boards, dry and dusty. Near it,
there was a magnificent six-foot-long Indian war bonnet
with eagle feathers and a bright pattern of beads the full

length of it. Tagg wondered drowsily where the bonnet came from.

"Go to sleep, dear." Annie blew out the tall kerosene lamp on the bureau, and Tagg settled down with a final wiggle between the crisp, cool sheets. He was fast asleep, even before Annie had softly closed the door and gone back to sit with Uncle Luke in front of the fire.

The logs had burned almost to ashes and still the two of them sat and talked. There was so much he wanted her to know about her mother's girlhood days on the old ranch, and about the years since then. And in turn, Annie had a lot to tell him about her father and his visits to her and Tagg, and finally about the long journey here.

"I still can't figure how you two kids did it, without a man along to give you a hand," the sheriff marveled.

"Guess we were just lucky," Annie smiled.

Sheriff Luke leaned over to poke up the fire. The governor's letter in his pocket crackled, and reminded him of his own troubles. He shook his head and sighed. "I hope you brought some of that luck along with you, honey. The way things have been going, I may have to give up my badge."

Annie laid her small strong hand on his arm. "I heard some talk about it back at Smoke Tree Station. But your friend, Mr. Castle, blamed it on politics." She looked searchingly into her uncle's face.

His eyes, so like Tagg's, were troubled as he stared into the flickering fire. When he spoke, he was weighing his words carefully. "I wonder. If it's only that, I reckon I haven't much kick coming. I've had the job a long spell, maybe too long, like they say."

"How does that man we met—that Mr. Shanley—feel about it?"

"John stands by me. He talks 'em down every time. He's a real friend, Annie."

"It's good you have somebody to bank on." Annie was indignant. "People are so ungrateful."

"I reckon you have to expect it, in my job."

"Well, they better not say anything against you while I'm listening. I'll soon put them straight!" Her blue eyes flashed so indignantly that the sheriff had to smile.

"You sound just like your mother," he chuckled, "when she used to argue with Pa about riding out alone. She was never scared of the Indians. Why, she had those squaws followin' her around like she was a queen or somethin'! She'd go right into their villages and hobnob with the chief himself, and she took care of the young 'uns when they

came down sick. That war bonnet in Tagg's room, Chief
Spotted Wing took that right off his own head and put
it on hers after she nursed his little girl out of pneumonia.
She—" He broke off abruptly and listened. "Somebody
coming. Riding fast."

Now Annie could hear the pounding of hoofs coming
nearer. Sheriff Luke started for the front door, taking a
lighted lamp from its bracket. "Uncle!" Annie remembered
the stories he had just told her about the outlaw raids.
"Please be careful!" If he opened that door with a lamp in
his hand he would be a perfect target!

Luke looked startled, then pleased. He set the lamp down
and blew out the light. "You've got a head on your shoulders, Annie," he told her. "Reckon I have been gettin' a
mite careless."

The rider was pulling up in the yard as the sheriff
cautiously opened the door and peered out.

"It's Lofty!" he exclaimed, and hurried out to meet the
young deputy as he dismounted at the porch.

Lofty's head was bandaged, and he was unsteady on his
feet as Luke took him by the arm and led him inside.

"What happened to you?" the sheriff demanded. "Who
hit you?"

Lofty told them about Rufe's trick and his escape. As he concluded, Annie spoke up excitedly. "Whoever came in the front door must have been the other masked man who was with him on the trail."

"More than likely!" Luke looked glum. "Well, I suppose anybody would have been fooled by Rufe's goings on, Lofty. There's no use cryin' over what's done. Tomorrow morning we'll try to pick up some kind of a trail and start after the two of them."

Lofty groaned and held his head. "You haven't heard the worst part yet." And he told them that while he was lying unconscious on the jail floor, somebody had put a half-empty liquor bottle and two glasses on the table, and had scattered his deck of cards around, so it looked as if he had been drinking and gambling with Horton, instead of guarding him properly. He had just come to his senses, and was getting up off the floor, when the town butcher had looked in to see why the jail door was standing open so late at night, and no lamp lit inside. Before Lofty had told half his story to the butcher, the room was swarming with men, most of them from the café across the street. And from the way they talked, Lofty knew that most of them were sure he was lying to save his own skin.

A few of the men had taken the prisoner's escape as a joke on the deputy, but others had been angry, and openly accused him of conniving to let the outlaw get away. Ben Crane, the mine owner, had done the loudest talking along those lines, Lofty admitted.

"Ben Crane," Annie told herself firmly, "I'll remember his name. He certainly isn't a friend of Uncle Luke's."

"I guess Ben's still pretty sore about losing part of his ore shipment last month." Luke shook his head sadly. "We never did find hide nor hair of the men who raided it."

"Uncle Luke," Annie was very serious, "why don't I go into town with you in the morning and see if I can pick up that feller's trail? I'm pretty good at tracking."

"Well, now, honey—" the sheriff flashed an uncertain glance at Lofty, who was frowning down at Annie, "it's right nice of you to offer, but—"

Lofty interrupted him. "You'd better rest up after your long trip, Miss Annie." She knew he was talking down to her, a mere girl. "I think we men folks can handle that end of it alone."

Annie's eyes sparked, and she opened her mouth to tell him off, but just then she caught the twinkle in Uncle Luke's eye, and she decided against it. Instead, she smiled meekly at the tall deputy and said, "I'm sure you can, Mr. Craig. I didn't mean that you needed my help." She grinned at her uncle. "Besides, I've got some housekeeping to do, haven't I, Uncle Luke? That'll keep me busy!" He nodded and gave her an understanding smile that Lofty missed completely.

Later, as she got ready for bed in the room that had been her mother's for so long, she smiled to recollect how she had worried about her uncle's honesty, till she had met him. Then she had suspected his deputy might be tied up with the outlaws. Well, thank goodness, she had been wrong about both of them. Lofty was a big friendly fellow, just the kind to be fooled by a mean customer like Rufe Horton. But, now, she had another name in her mind—Ben Crane. She thought sleepily, "I wonder if Crane wants to give the sheriff job to some friend of his. Maybe that's why he's so angry with Uncle Luke. I think I'll ask that nice Mr. Shanley what he thinks about it, next time I see him."

Even as Annie was turning out the lamp in her ranch bedroom, "that nice Mr. Shanley" was admitting a visitor at the side door of his mansion in Diablo. The two men moved through the dark hall to Shanley's elegantly furnished library.

It wasn't the first time Dude Rango had reported to his boss in the middle of the night. He usually came to bring news of a successful holdup carried out, or to collect for an earlier one. This time, John Shanley had sent word to him by Rube Horton.

Shanley closed the library door firmly. The two house servants had retired several hours ago, but there was always a chance that they might hear voices and come downstairs to listen. He didn't intend to pay blackmail.

The sharp-featured young outlaw was better dressed than the Horton twins. He had earned his nickname of "Dude" because of his fondness for fine silk 'shirts and hundred-dollar riding boots. He was slim and wiry, with the smooth graceful movements of a mountain lion. And he was just as treacherous.

While the Hortons were out-and-out roughnecks, and addicted to gun-waving and loud talk, Dude Rango was quiet and soft-spoken most of the time. He was unknown in Diablo, but back in the part of the Territory where he came from, they knew him as a hot-tempered gunslinger. It had been rumored that he had "gone bad" because of some tragedy in his boyhood that had turned him against law and order, but the plain truth was that he had chosen crime quite deliberately. He had a lazy streak, and it was easier to grab the luxuries he craved, through holdups and crooked gambling, than it was to work honestly for them. In that way, he was like many another legendary gunman of the time.

Rango worked for John Shanley because he liked hand-worked silver-trimmed boots with Mexican silver spurs, and not because he had any respect for his employer. He swung the boots up onto the polished mahogany desk, and leaned back in the expensive leather chair. "What's bothering you now?" he asked lazily.

Shanley scowled at the boots on his desk. "I ran into some bad news today," he began. "I found out why MacTavish has been so stubborn about holding onto his ranch. The old fool has brought his niece and nephew out here to live with him."

"Yeah." Dude swung his feet down so he could reach over and help himself to a handful of Havana cigars from the silver-bound humidor on the desk. "So Rube was telling me. Seems to me it's about time you quit coddling Mac-Tavish and took my advice."

John Shanley paced the floor. "I don't like to go that far. Besides, what good would it do to kill him, when he still holds title to the ranch? It's the ranch I've got to have, and it has to be mine legally."

"I still say get rid of him, and then come up with a handful of I.O.U.'s against the property. I'm pretty good at copying handwriting. I'll fix 'em up. It's quick and sure."

Shanley scowled. "I can't afford to take a chance. He's no gambler, so why would he give me I.O.U's?"

"Agh!" Rango shrugged it away. "You're smart enough to think up an answer to that."

"Maybe so, maybe not. Meantime, I'm going to try something else. I've sent for my daughter Edith. I'll get her and this niece of Luke's together. Edith'll go to work on her. She'll show off her fancy clothes, and keep harping on what fun she has at her school, and what pals they'd be if they could be there together. I'll lay a bet Edith can make her so sour on that run-down ranch, she'll be after Luke in no time to sell it and let her go East this fall. I'll put in my two cents at the same time, with Luke."

"Yeah, but what about the boy? He might like the ranch."

"He's just a kid. It's the girl Luke would listen to. Seems she reminds him of her mother."

"It could work, but you have less than three months to

get that ranch in your name, and divided into the lots you sold those settlers. I still say my idea's the only sure answer." He ran a finger expressively under his throat in a gesture of cutting that made John Shanley wince.

"I'll give mine a good try first," Shanley insisted. "If it doesn't work out, why—" he left the rest unsaid.

Dude nodded. "Don't stall too long," he advised, "or you'll wish you hadn't. Meanwhile, do we keep on making things lively around Diablo? Crane's payroll up at the mine is pretty hefty now."

"Go ahead. But be careful. I hear Luke's niece is a dead shot. Rube claims she knocked the guns out of his hands."

Rango snorted. "That's *his* story. She probably made a lucky shot, and he and Rufe lost their nerve and let her take over."

"Well," Shanley wanted to believe it, "anyhow, tell them not to let her get a chance to practice on them again."

8                            New Friends

Annie was up at sunrise. This day would be a busy one. They had to unload the wagon and settle the few pieces of furniture they had brought with them across country. She tiptoed to the kitchen, hoping she wouldn't awaken either Uncle Luke or Tagg.

There stood the new wood stove that Uncle Luke had written about. It was the very latest word in luxury, with its solid black top, polished till it shone. There were four big cooking holes, each covered with an iron lid. And the word HOME glowed at her in shining metal letters from the oven door. But—most wonderful of all—there was a deep well at one side of the iron beauty, filled with water, that would get hot as the stove warmed up! Uncle Luke had a neat pile of firewood beside the stove, and had laid a fire that needed only one of the sulphur matches from the ironstone match holder above the stove, to set it blazing.

Across the big room, the open fireplace looked deserted and forlorn. A three-legged, soot-blackened kettle hung on its hook over the clean-swept hearth, and there was thick dust on the old leather bellows that leaned dejectedly against the brick frame. She thought of the hundreds of good hearty meals that had been cooked in that big old fireplace, long before there was a stove in the Territory. Now it was good only for extra use when the handsome new iron stove was too crowded.

She soon had the big coffeepot steaming and a tall stack of flapjacks keeping warm on the back of the stove.

Uncle Luke poked a smiling face through the doorway from the hall. "I heard something going on," he chuckled, "but I figured it was mice."

Annie waved a big iron mixing spoon. "It better not be, in *my* kitchen!"

He sniffed the air with approval. "Somethin' smells like real coffee!" He poked an exploratory finger into the top flapjack. "Real gentle little critters," he decided, "they don't snap back like mine do!"

Annie laughed and filled his plate. "Did you hear Tagg stirring in there, Uncle Luke?"

"Not a sound. Guess the little feller's still tired. We better let him sleep till—"

A high-pitched yell came from somewhere outside. "Hey, Annie! Come and look!"

Annie dropped the spoon and ran to the back door. Tagg, in his night clothes, was galloping a handsome black and white pony across the rear yard. When he reached the far end, he wheeled it and came dashing back.

"Well, I'll be jiggered!" Uncle Luke slapped his thigh and chuckled.

Tagg pulled up with a flourish at the back door. "I found my pony! In the barn!" He shouted at Annie. "Isn't he a beaut?"

"I'll pony you, young man, if you don't get in here this minute and put your clothes on!"

Tagg knew that tone of voice. He dismounted hastily, but stood with his arm around the pony's neck.

"He *is* the one you promised me, isn't he, Uncle Luke?"

The big man laughed. "He sure is, Tagg. He's been waitin' quite a while for you."

Tagg laid his cheek against the pony's soft neck. "I just love him," he said solemnly. "And thanks, Uncle Luke. Thanks a whole lot."

"Now take him back to the barn," Annie tried to keep her voice stern, "and then you hike right back here and get ready for your breakfast."

When he was out of hearing, she laughed. "He's been talking about that pony for two months. I guess he just couldn't wait!"

"I never figured he'd be up at the crack of dawn, or I'd've been right there in the barn to introduce the two of them!" He chuckled.

She grinned in return. "It looks like they tended to that themselves!"

The ranch was small, but there was everything on it that a curious small boy and an adventure-loving girl could ask for. While Luke MacTavish and Lofty Craig were trying, with no success, to trace the escaped prisoner and his rescuer, Annie and Tagg had a wonderful time exploring the far corners of the ranch. Luke had only a few range cattle, and one milk cow, so there was little outside work to do, and they had a lot of time on their hands.

Tagg added some rare items to his collection of odds and ends. Annie was willing to let him keep most of his new-found treasures, but things like dead scorpions had

a way of disappearing out of his room without much delay. He didn't mind. There were plenty more!

They were resting on the top step of the shady front porch one afternoon later in the week. Annie's horse, Target, and the pony—which Tagg had promptly named Pixie—were dozing under the big tree beside the well, saddled and waiting for their last canter of the day.

Annie looked with a critical eye at the discarded snake-skin that was Tagg's latest find. "You have three of those things now," she wrinkled her nose and carefully avoided touching it, "I should think that would be almost enough for anybody."

"But I want to send one back to Aunt Martha and Cousin Emily and—" he ticked them off on his fingers.

"I can just see their faces when they open the package!" Annie laughed.

Tagg looked reproachful, but his attention was switched suddenly to a buckboard coming along the ranch road. He jumped up and shaded his eyes. "It's that Mr. Shanley we met in Diablo! And there's a dressed-up lady with him!" He squinted. "Golly, I'll bet that's his daughter he was telling you about!"

Annie rose quickly and brushed the dust off her riding

skirt and jacket. She was excited and happy at the idea of meeting a girl somewhere near her own age. Tagg was a darling, of course, but after all, he was just a little boy. She hoped Edith Shanley would like to ride and hike. She had made a few friends back in the Middle West in public school, but she had been sort of tied down taking care of Tagg; and they never had become close pals. But with Mr. Shanley and Uncle Luke so friendly, maybe she and Edith would hit it off the same way.

In the front seat of the shiny buckboard with its fringed top, John Shanley was speaking a last word of caution to his daughter.

"Get a smile on your face, miss," he said sharply. "I want her to like you."

Edith Shanley's brown eyes smouldered. She turned her pretty, delicately moulded face toward her father. "How is this?" she asked, twisting her cupid's-bow lips into an artificial smirk.

John Shanley scowled and glanced quickly toward the two figures on the distant porch. "Listen to me," he said quickly. "I dislike all this just as much as you do, but it has to be done. Let me remind you that unless I can get legal title to this ranch before fall, I'm going to prison! And you know what that will do to you."

Edith's eyes flashed. "How you ever got yourself into such a stupid position—" She left the rest unsaid, because they were close to the house now, and Annie was coming down the steps to meet them, with Tagg close behind her.

John Shanley pulled in the high-stepping horses, and waved his carriage whip in greeting. "Hello, there!" he called genially. And under his breath, he told Edith, "Now, remember!"

Tagg stood back bashfully, as Shanley helped his daughter down and introduced the two girls. They were a striking contrast. Edith was a tiny thing, half a head shorter than Annie, and her fashionable silk dress, puffed and frilled, and trimmed with yards of delicate lace, was almost the shade of her reddish-brown hair. Her tiny hat perched on a mass of curls, and a feather plume swept stylishly down beside her pink and white cheek. She gave a lace-gloved hand to Annie who took it in a firm, friendly clasp.

"Papa has been telling me how brave you were, making that long hard journey all by yourself," she smiled up into Annie's honest blue eyes.

"I was along," Tagg explained. His freckled face was very serious.

"You certainly were, button!" Annie pulled him over and hugged him as she introduced him to Edith.

"Well, no wonder you weren't afraid!" Edith giggled and showed her dimples. Then and there, Tagg decided that Miss Shanley was not only the prettiest but the nicest young lady he had ever met—next to Annie, of course.

They all moved up onto the porch, where Annie made the Shanleys comfortable and brought them refreshingly cool water from the old well. Edith was a pretty picture in her fashionable outfit, and Annie admired it without envy. Her one "Sunday dress" had long since been outgrown, and she had never thought of replacing it. There were too many other uses for what little money she and Tagg had.

"Well, my dear," Shanley smiled fondly at his daughter, "I think we'll be starting home, as soon as you tell Miss Oakley one of the reasons we came this afternoon."

"Of course, Papa!" Edith was the sweetly affectionate little daughter. She had been chattering on about her friends and her school and her plans for the fall. Annie and Tagg had seemed to be very much impressed.

"It's a party," she confided prettily, "a lawn party Friday at our house. There'll be Japanese lanterns and ice cream and—oh, all sorts of surprises! I'd love to have you come."

"I've already talked to your uncle," Shanley explained genially, "and he agrees that it'd be a good chance for you to meet all the substantial Diablo folks at one time. Sort of a welcome party for you."

"Why, thank you! That would be lovely!"

Edith was on her feet, opening her tiny, lace-trimmed parasol for the short walk to the buckboard.

"We'll have a wonderful time," she told Annie. Then she noticed Tagg's long face. "Oh—and we'll need somebody to help make the ice cream, won't we, Papa?"

"Why not?" Shanley winked at Annie. "A strong boy to turn the handle on the freezer."

"Can I, Annie? Please?" Tagg looked as if his whole future hung on the answer. Annie nodded. Tagg whooped and dashed down the steps to stand on his head. Edith's gay little laugh tinkled, and Tagg was so happy that he ran over to Pixie and made a fast mount.

John Shanley helped Edith into the buckboard and started around to the other side. He was pleased with how well everything seemed to have gone, and pleased with Edith for playing up to both the Oakleys.

Over beside the well, Tagg gathered Pixie's reins and

wheeled him toward the buckboard. With a sudden un-
earthly screech that was his own version of an Indian
war whoop, he dug his heels into the little pony's flanks,
and took off at a gallop straight across in front of Shanley's
high-stepping carriage horses.

One of them reared violently, and there was the sound of
a snapping rein. Edith screamed. Now both horses took
fright, rearing and plunging, and before John Shanley
could get around to the driver's seat to grab the flying reins,
the animals had started to run. Edith shrieked again and
tumbled off the seat to the floor in a confusion of lace ruffles,
curls, and feathers, as the team broke into a runaway gallop.

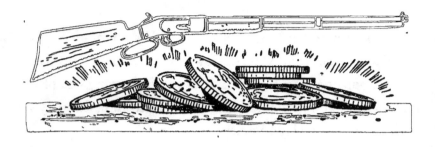

# 9            The Rescue

Annie made a flying mount on Target and raced to stop the runaway team before they could reach the open gates. In the buckboard, Edith was being bounced about helplessly, too terrified now even to scream.

Shanley stood frozen, expecting his daughter to be thrown out of the swaying wagon at any moment; while Tagg, horrified at what he had done, watched helplessly.

Annie had almost reached the side of the buckboard when it swung around and out into the open road, but the scared thoroughbreds pulled away fast from the slower cow pony. Annie yelled "Whoa!" and rode hard to try to head them off, but she was losing ground rapidly.

Edith clawed her way up off the floor of the buckboard and tried desperately to catch the loosely flying reins, but they whipped past her.

Now the buckboard swung around a turn in the narrow road, and Edith screamed and cowered down against the seat as she saw a heavily loaded hay wagon ahead. It was moving slowly, and it filled the road from one side ditch to the other. There was no chance for the runaways to pass it. In another moment, the buckboard would crash into its heavy wooden tail gate.

Then a rope sailed past her and circled the neck of the left-hand runaway. It tightened and pulled him back violently, breaking his stride. Edith looked back to see Annie, riding hard, with the rope snubbed on her saddle.

She was keeping the rope taut, hauling it in, hand over hand, as she brought the runaways gradually under control with Target's help. Now the cow pony dug in his forefeet and braced himself hard, and up ahead, the nearer horse was pulled almost to a stop. Still keeping the rope tight, in spite of the big thoroughbred's frightened plunging, Annie grabbed his bit and pulled him to a full stop. His mate kicked frantically against the restraint for a moment, and then subsided.

By the time John Shanley had come up, to lift the bedraggled Edith out of the buckboard, Annie had both horses quieted. Up ahead, the hay wagon lumbered on.

Edith's pretty nose was scratched, and her elegant feather hung down over one eye at a rakish angle. The lace-trimmed gown was ripped, and the stylish parasol had a broken handle. But that was nothing to what had happened to Edith's temper. It was completely fractured. She glared at Tagg, as the scared boy rode up and swung off his pony.

He could see that Edith was furious. "I—I'm sorry I spooked 'em, Miss Shanley," he stammered. "I sure didn't mean to."

Her father's warning grip on her arm made Edith swallow her angry words before they could come out.

"We know you didn't mean to frighten the horses," John Shanley spoke hurriedly. "Edith understands that, don't you, dear?"

"Of course!" Edith had recovered her self-control. She smiled with an effort and patted Tagg's head.

"Golly, thank you, Miss Shanley. I guess most folks would be awful sore. You're swell!"

"Forget it, sonny." John Shanley put a lot of warmth into it, and as Annie came up, he turned to her and took both her hands in his. "If it hadn't been for you," he told her, with an effective break in his voice, "my little girl might have been badly hurt. I won't forget this!"

When the Shanleys were once more on their way back to town, Annie spoke sternly to her small brother. It was a voice she seldom used. "I hope this will teach you to quit trying to show off, Tagg."

"I'm sorry, Sis," Tagg lowered his chin. "I was just so glad about going to the party."

"I know, honey," Annie couldn't be angry with him for long. "We won't say any more about it. If they could forgive you the way they did, I guess I can, too."

In the buckboard, Edith Shanley sat bolt upright at her father's side. The drooping feather swung down against her cheek, and she slapped it aside angrily.

He stole a look at her before he spoke. He could see she was in a temper. "What do you think of MacTavish's niece?" he ventured.

"I don't like her, and I don't intend to put myself out being nice to her! If she comes to the party, after *this*, I intend to ignore her!"

"I don't think so, Edith." Shanley's tone matched hers.

"Just watch!" she snapped. "I'll take her down a peg . . . her and that brother of hers, the nasty little—"

"That's enough!" John Shanley's voice cut like a lash. For a few minutes they rode on in silence. Then Shanley spoke, quietly. "I'll make a bargain with you. What was it you wrote me about Senator Brown's daughter going to Paris next winter?"

Edith's face brightened. "She's leaving in December. Why?"

"Simply this: If you'll help me with these Oakleys, and I get that ranch in my name, I'll have money to burn. I'll send you to Paris with the Brown girl, and I'll double your allowance—I'll triple it."

Edith studied his face shrewdly. "I'll need a whole new wardrobe if I go abroad."

"You shall have it," he agreed.

"All right, then. I'll do what I can, but I don't know how long I can stand those two."

"We'll get it over with as soon as possible," he promised, and added, "this little near-accident was lucky for us. I know how I can make good use of it, with your help. Now, at the party—" and he outlined a plan of action.

Back at the Bull's-Eye, Tagg sat on the steps lost in deep thought. Annie came out with a bowl of peas and a cooking pot, and plunked them down beside him. "Get busy there, young feller," she nudged him, "or supper's going to be late." She sat down on the other side of the bowl and started to shell.

"Hi, there, kids!" It was Uncle Luke, looking tired. He sat down heavily in the rickety old porch chair.

"Any news about the prisoner?" Annie asked.

"Not a trace. Seems nobody ever even heard his name before."

"Mr. Shanley and his daughter were here," Annie began.

"So I just heard in 'town," Luke interrupted. "The whole shebang is buzzing about your roping down the runaway team. Shanley's saying that you saved Edith's life. What's the straight of it?"

Annie explained, while Tagg sat miserably silent and red-faced under the sheriff's stern eye. At the end Luke nodded gravely. "Good work, Annie. Sounds like Shanley wasn't stretching it, at that. He swears he's going to do something handsome for you as a reward."

Annie brushed the idea aside. "Tell him to forget that." Then she grinned happily. "Did he tell you about the lawn party they're giving Friday?"

Luke chuckled. "He sure did! It looks like the whole county will be turning out to meet you!" He had a sobering thought. "Except a few, like Ben Crane, who don't have much use for me any more."

"I wouldn't care to meet that kind, anyhow!" Annie tossed her neat little braids.

"Oh, big Ben's all right. He's just hotheaded." Luke sighed and shrugged his shoulders. "He never means half he says he does."

"What does Mr. Shanley think of him?"

"I never asked him about it," Luke answered, carelessly. "Like to make up my own mind about folks." Then, "By jingo, I just remembered, honey. Miss Edith said to tell you she'd be wearin' a white party dress for the shindig, an' she thought it would be right cute if you did, too."

"A white party dress?" Annie looked dismayed. "I don't have one! In fact, I don't have *any* kind of a party dress. I forgot I'd have to fix up, when I told her I'd be there."

"Wear whatever you've got, then!" Uncle Luke solved her problem in typical male fashion. "It's you the folks want to meet, not your clothes!"

"No, Uncle Luke. I can't go."

"But the party's for *you!*"

"All the more reason why I'm not going without looking right!"

Luke was baffled. He saw that his usually amiable niece

was in deadly earnest. He glanced over to Tagg for support, but Tagg wore a blank expression. He would be no help. Suddenly the big man's eyes lighted up. "White dress!" he repeated. "I know where there's a white dress!"

"You do?" Annie gasped. "Where, Uncle Luke? Whose? Would it fit me?"

"Come on and I'll show you where it is." He smiled and crooked a finger at her as he started into the house, Annie after him like a flash.

A small trunk with a rounded lid stood in the corner of Annie's room. She hadn't paid much attention to it, because it had a colorful Navaho blanket thrown over it, and there was a jumble of Indian baskets piled on top. Now Luke swept aside the baskets and blanket, and knelt to open the little trunk.

"Last time this was opened," he told Annie as he turned the key in the rusty lock, "your mother put away her wedding dress and veil. She gave me the key just before they drove off on their honeymoon. I recollect what she said, out at the carriage. 'Some day I'll come back for it,' she told me, 'when Jared and I are settled on a place of our own. But if I don't, I want you to keep it for one of our daughters. We're going to have seven at least!' "

He lifted out the fragile satin gown, a little yellowed by time, but still exquisitely soft and rich. The lace fell in delicate folds across his big rough hands, and Annie hurried to take it gently into her own and hold it reverently. "It's lovely," she said, softly. Then she held it up to her, and crossed to the tall pier glass to catch a full-length view. She stared at herself with misty eyes, as the faint fragrance of violet perfume that still clung to it brought back memories of a tall, golden-haired girl with a gay, smiling face, who used to romp with her.

"Well," the sheriff boomed genially, "will it do?"

"Oh, Uncle Luke, it's absolutely perfect! I'll just have to shorten it a little."

"You'll be the belle of the ball," he chuckled. "And now, how about supper for a couple of starving ranch hands?"

# 10             The Lawn Party

The Shanley garden, with its precious green lawn that cost John Shanley so much to maintain, was in gala dress. From one tall tree to the next, the servants had strung Japanese paper lanterns, each with a candle inside that would be lighted when the sun had gone down. Crepe paper and bunting festooned the wide, shady porch, and more Japanese lanterns swung there. The ornate iron gates stood wide to receive the awed Diabloites who had already started arriving in carriages, buckboards, ranch wagons, and on horseback.

Under the trees, long pine tables were being spread with checkered homespun tablecloths, and there was a procession of kitchen help bringing out great round silver platters of dainty sandwiches and tall frosted layer cakes, decorated with pink and white rosebuds and spun-sugar curlicues.

And for the menfolks, there were huge apple pies, brown-crusted and steaming from the oven. But the most impressive sight to greet the eyes of the guests was the huge silver punch bowl, filled with fruited lemonade, and set in a washtub crammed to the brim with ice—real ice!

Shanley had sent all the way to Bonanza City for that ice—twenty miles away. Half of it had melted on the road, but there was still enough left to cool the lemonade, freeze the ice cream, and furnish the Diablo citizens with a topic of conversation for months to come!

Edith still lingered in her room, adding final touches to her toilette. She smiled approvingly at herself in the long mirror. Her wide-skirted white party dress was as becoming as she had hoped, but she was a little pale. She remedied that by pinching her cheeks till they turned pink. The added color was very pretty, she decided. But when she got to Paris, she would buy some of that naughty stuff called rouge, that the heroines in all the paper-backed novels seemed to use.

"Hurry, Edith. People are getting here." Her father stood frowning in the doorway. "I want you to be there when the Oakleys and MacTavish arrive."

"I will, Papa—dear," she drawled, pirouetting languidly

in front of the mirror. "I can hardly wait to see that Oakley
girl in her idea of a party dress! I hope I can keep from
giggling!"

"See that you do!" Shanley reminded her sharply. "Save
your giggles till after I have MacTavish's signature on a
deed to that ranch of his!"

Edith ran to the window. There was a commotion down
on the lawn. Someone was being greeted loudly, and it even
sounded like a cheer or two. She stared down through the
heavy lace curtains.

Sheriff Luke had pulled in through the tall iron gates
in his old squeaking-wheeled ranch wagon. He was driving,
and Annie and Tagg sat beside him. The cheers were evidently for her. She was wearing a long, old-fashioned cape
with a hood and Edith couldn't make out what her dress
was like.

She saw several of the men bring their ladies forward
to meet the sheriff's niece, as Luke helped his "family"
down from the wagon. A moment later, Annie was out of
sight in the crowd. Edith's face was twisted in a sarcastic
smile as she turned abruptly from the window to her father.

"Your guest of honor has arrived," she said. "Let's go
down and join the worshipers." She couldn't help a final

dig at her father. "In spite of your campaign, Papa, dear, MacTavish still seems to have quite a few friends in Diablo."

Shanley nodded. "Not as many as he used to have. Just do your part with the girl and I'll take care of MacTavish."

Annie still wore the long cloak over her dress as Edith drew her over to kiss her on the cheek. "I'm so happy you came," she exclaimed, then she whispered, "I was afraid my silly message about wearing a white dress might have upset you, if you didn't happen to have one. I'm sure you'll be adorable in anything you've worn."

Annie smiled and unfastened her long wrap. "I *was* sort of worried for a few minutes," she admitted frankly, "but Uncle Luke found this for me." She threw off the cloak and revealed the softly gleaming wedding satin. Edith's gasp of surprise was echoed by the admiring murmurs of the guests around them.

Edith's own gown was pretty, but Annie's had yards more material—and a train! She could have choked the sheriff's niece with her bare hands! Instead, she had to smile and gurgle, "How charming! and the latest style, too!"

Annie grinned. "It's not so late, I'm afraid. It was my mother's wedding gown, and it's been in her trunk at the ranch for nearly twenty years, Uncle Luke says."

"I remember the wedding!" It was Jake Karney who owned the general store in Diablo. "Your pa was in his cavalry uniform, sword an' all. We shivareed 'em!"

Annie looked startled and turned to Uncle Luke for an explanation. He was laughing. "That's right, Jake! We sure did!" He told Annie, "It was an old custom hereabouts. Don't do it much any more. Serenaded the newlyweds and played tricks on 'em. Called it shivaree-ing." He chuckled.

Edith smiled coldly. "We'll have to hear more about the pioneer customs later," she said lightly. "Right now, I believe the refreshments are ready." She slipped her silk-mittened hand through the sheriff's arm, and led the way toward the tables.

Annie glanced around for Tagg, but he had disappeared into the kitchen, where he was valiantly at work turning the handle of the ice-cream freezer. It was a hard job, but every small boy tried to get it, because whoever did it, afterward got to lick the paddles, all encrusted with thick, rich, gooey cream.

John Shanley offered Annie his arm, and strolled slowly with her toward the buzzing crowd around the tables. This was the opportunity he had been waiting for. "I've been wondering how I could best thank you for saving my girl's life in the runaway," he began.

"Please," Annie spoke quickly, "forget it! Tagg made the horses run away, with his nonsense, and it's thanks enough if you forgive him for it."

"We already have, my dear! All boys are full of high spirits."

"It's right nice of you and Edith to feel that way. Tagg'll be happy to hear it."

"I hope *you* will be happy when I tell you what Edith and I want to do to show our gratitude."

They were on the fringe of the chattering guests now, and Shanley drew Annie toward her uncle, as he called: "Luke! Come here, will you?"

Sheriff Luke sauntered over with a glass of lemonade in one hand and a large sandwich in the other. "What's she been doing now?" he joked. "Breakin' the law?"

"Luke," Shanley's voice was impressive, "what would you say to sending this girl of yours to the best finishing school in the East, the one Edith goes to?"

Luke and Annie were equally surprised. "It's Edith's own idea," Shanley continued, "and she's dead set on it since Annie saved her life the other day. She wants Annie to have all the best that there is."

Luke shook his head slowly. "It's what I'd like for her, John, but I can't swing it. I'm not a rich man like you."

"You misunderstand, old friend," John Shanley put his arm over the tall sheriff's shoulders. "I'll take care of all the expenses. It's the only way Edith and I could think up to show how grateful we are to Annie."

"Can't let you do it." MacTavish was firm.

"Of course not!" Annie smiled. "But it was sweet of Edith to think of it, just the same."

"Now, wait!" Shanley held them both. "I won't let you say no. The amount of money it'll take is only about the price I get for one small lot; and, anyhow, it's just lying in the bank doing nobody any good."

The sheriff still shook his head. Shanley turned to Annie. "Annie, make this old mossback listen to reason! Tell him how selfish he is keeping you cooped up on a ranch away out here, instead of having fun like other girls your age!"

"But I like the ranch, Mr. Shanley." She met her uncle's questioning look with a reassuring nod. "I hate to seem ungrateful, but I don't want to go away from here. This is home. And Tagg and I are happy on the ranch."

"Edith!" Shanley beckoned to his daughter. "These

stubborn people won't listen to our little plan. See if you can change their minds."

"Please—pretty please?" Edith used her best smile as she looked appealingly at the sheriff. "Let Annie come to school with me! We'll have so much fun together!" She turned to Annie. "I know you don't want to stay here on a horrid little old ranch, when you could visit Paris!"

"Paris?" Annie turned to Shanley, surprised.

"Of course!" Edith bubbled on. "Didn't Papa tell you that he wants to send the both of us to Paris during winter vacation?"

"I didn't get to it," Shanley laughed, "but I was just about to!" He was glad Edith had thought that one up. Annie's eyes were sparkling with interest. Maybe that was the bait they needed.

"You will come, won't you?" Edith babbled, clutching Annie's arm and smiling appealingly into her eyes. "Some of the girls are going, too. You'll just love Senator Brown's daughter, and the governor's niece!"

Annie shook her head. "I'm afraid not," she said soberly. "I belong here. I didn't really know it till I put on this dress of Mother's. It's pretty and all, but I don't feel comfortable dressed up. I guess I was cut out for plain ranch life."

Edith pouted and stamped her foot. "Oh, dear!" she wailed, "I was counting on showing you off to the girls!" To herself, she thought, "Ugh! I can imagine!" but she kept a bright smile going.

"If I had the money right now," Sheriff Luke told them, "I'd make Annie go along back to school with you, Miss Edith. She's never had time to take it easy and have fun, like most other girls. But it's not our habit to let others foot our bills, on *any* excuse!"

"Uncle's right," Annie smiled.

"Well," Edith dimpled at them, "there's still time to change your minds. I'll keep on hoping till the day before I have to leave for school." She gathered up her long skirts with one hand, threw the sheriff and Annie a kiss with the other, and skipped back to her other guests.

Shanley tried to keep smiling pleasantly. "We'll hold it open. I won't take no for an answer yet."

When he had followed Edith, Annie turned to her uncle and was surprised to see him looking glum. "Why, what's bothering you, Uncle Luke?"

"I was just wondering if I should have sold that old rundown ranch of ours to Shanley, long ago, when he offered to buy it. I reckon it isn't a place for a growing-up girl, at that.

If I'd sold, I'd have the money to give you the things other girls have."

"Uncle Luke!" Annie's eyes flashed and she looked almost angry. "I meant what I said to them about the ranch being where I want to stay. I love it. And I don't want to go away to school or Paris or any other place. I want to be here where I have a real home, the sort of home that Dad and Mother used to plan for. You believe me, don't you, Uncle Luke?"

"I think I do, honey," the big man nodded slowly. "And I'm right glad to hear it. It reminds me of somethin' I've been wantin' to do for a long time and, by jing, I'm going to tend to it the next time Judge Berry holds court at Bonanza City!" He wouldn't say what it was, but his eyes twinkled and he seemed highly pleased at his decision.

Inside the big house, the strains of a fiddle and a guitar announced that dancing was under way. A caller bellowed, "Grab yore ladies for a Virginia Reel!" And the guests started crowding in. The big entrance hall had been cleared so the dancers would have plenty of room, and they were soon stamping out the figures of the reel, the square dances, and the Paul Jones, with noise and enthusiasm. Those who didn't care to dance kept busy with gossip and chatter around the refreshment tables inside and out. And when the big lemonade bowl was empty, it was quickly refilled, and the house rang with music and laughter. It was a most successful party.

All evening, Annie had to tell about her experiences along the overland trail. Tagg, puffed with too much ice cream, shone in her reflected glory, and was there to remind her of incidents she forgot to mention. Altogether, it was Annie's party. And Edith Shanley hated every minute of it. But she was the one who urged her to tell more.

"Tell us about that awful horse thief!" she begged. And Annie couldn't refuse.

"It's too bad he got away." Edith shuddered delicately. "I'm scared to drive even a half mile from home now!"

"I doubt if you're in any danger, my dear," Shanley laughed. "That fellow'll steer clear of the Diablo ladies since he's had a taste of Annie's sharpshooting!"

"You really ought to make Annie a deputy, instead of that young man who was so careless," Edith's voice was raised so that it would reach most of the guests. Several of them drifted over to hear what was going on. Shanley answered loudly for their benefit.

"You don't know what you're talking, Edith," he said sharply. "He's a very reliable young man. He was tricked." He saw some frowns on the faces of the listeners. "There's too much loose talk going on against our lawmen. I, for one, am behind both Sheriff Luke here and his deputy, a hundred per cent!" He laid a hand on Luke's shoulder as he spoke.

There were murmurs of approval, and only a few growls of disagreement.

Sheriff Luke beamed at this loyal friend of his, and thought how lucky he was to have him. Edith giggled an apology and danced away, but they had stirred up doubts, she and her father, just as they had intended to do. And Shanley had managed to plant in everyone's mind the conviction that he was the sheriff's very good friend.

It was nearly midnight before the final lingering guest had driven noisily off in the last of the ranch wagons. Edith followed her father into the big reception hall. "Well, that's over!" she said crossly. "We tried. Now what do we do?"

"Now," he answered grimly, "I stop experimenting and go to work on them."

"How long do I have to stay around Diablo and be bored to death by its stupid villagers?" she demanded.

"Till I don't need you any longer," he snapped, "and watch yourself with Annie. I caught you scowling at her a couple of times. A lot depends on convincing her that we are very fond of her—*very* fond!" He stopped at the foot of the stairs. "And don't forget it!"

He stalked up to his room, and a few minutes later she was amazed to see him come down again wearing a riding outfit. "I'll be gone several hours," he told her.

"In the middle of the night?"

"My business won't wait. My dear friend the sheriff informed me tonight that he intends to deed his ranch over to Annie as soon as Circuit Judge Berry gets to Bonanza City for his regular session. And that may be any day now!"

"To *Annie!* Then you'll never have a chance of getting it! The dear thing's sentimental about her new home!"

"Maybe so," he smiled thinly, "but it isn't in her name *yet!*"

# *11*             The Trap Is Set

It was a long and dangerous ride that John Shanley took that midnight along the seldom used back trail to Jumpoff, high in the rugged desert hills. Dawn was in the sky as he turned a corner in the narrow trail and looked down into the sleeping town, far below, clinging to the steep mountainside.

There were no lights to be seen in any of the small cabins that perched on stilts above its narrow winding main street. Half-crumbled shacks and log cabins marked the edges of town, and only a handful of buildings in the very center of Jumpoff looked solid and usable. It was almost a ghost town now, but John Shanley remembered it when life there had teemed at fever pitch, and a string of mines all around the town had poured out fortunes as they tapped the big vein of gold quartz that seemed inexhaustible.

Then suddenly the tragedy so common in gold rush days had hit Jumpoff. They had lost the mother lode, the principal vein of rich gold-bearing quartz that was the life blood of the settlement. At first Jumpoff's citizens had refused to believe that the gold and their luck had run out. Most of them kept digging, but with waning hope, and when fresh discoveries were made one day on a distant ridge, they had stampeded off to the new claims, leaving household goods, even clothing and personal belongings, behind, abandoned.

Now Jumpoff was only a dingy way station on the old trail that meandered between Bonanza City at one end and far-off Silvertown on the other side of the range. It had four saloons, two livery stables, a ramshackle hotel, and a Chinese laundry. Most of the inhabitants made a sketchy living off the night-riding outlaws and other riffraff that drifted through, now broke and now well supplied with gold. It was feast or famine most of the time for many of Jumpoff's citizens.

But there were others who lived there for convenience—and were quite comfortable. There were advantages in living in an isolated spot like Jumpoff, where no questions were asked—and where the law was a good ten miles away in Diablo.

Shanley moved with the ease of long acquaintance down
the steep road into the dark main street. He pulled up
quietly in front of a small house whose front looked as
rickety and abandoned as the rest. From somewhere in the
back of the house, he heard a tenor voice singing rather
softly, a mournful ballad about a lone cowboy in the moonlight. He knew the voice. His trip hadn't been for nothing.
He made his way on foot to the back of the house, where
an upper window showed a light. He knocked on the door
and called softly, "Rango!"

The coal oil lamp inside went out suddenly and the
plaintive ballad stopped.

"Rango, it's me! Open up!" He raised his voice a little.

He could see a head stuck out of the upstairs window.
He stepped back from the doorway and waved. The head
was withdrawn, and a moment later the door opened, and
Shanley went inside.

When he left an hour later, he had made his deal with
Dude Rango in all the detail that the sleek young gunslinger had demanded. It was the same deal that Rango
had been urging all along, the one Shanley had put off in
favor of less violent methods. It was going to cost Shanley
more than he had planned, because now Rango knew that

he was desperate and had to move fast.

Upstairs in the small Jumpoff house, Dude Rango yawned and went to bed. He was very well pleased with the new arrangements. He would see the Hortons today and tell them what to do to earn their share.

John Shanley put spurs to the well-trained sorrel horse and headed back toward Diablo. It would be well into the day before he could get there, but he had long since established a habit of going for long rides "into the country" from time to time, and no one would question. Most of the Diabloites were under the impression that he was always scouting for new land to subdivide or new mining claims to buy up.

When he had gone a certain distance from Jumpoff, along the high winding trail, he spotted a big outcrop of rocks he had been watching for across the canyon. The early sun had come up above the high peaks by now, and the trail was clear in the daylight. It was not as wide as he had thought when he came over it during the night, and he felt his spine tingle as he moved gingerly over to the edge and stared down two hundred feet to the rocky floor. The canyon itself was narrow at this point, just as Dude had said, and there was an excellent spot among those big rocks directly opposite, where a man could lie in ambush and pick off a rider on this side. Yes, this was the perfect spot! He decided that maybe, after all, the thousand dollars he was paying Dude Rango and the Hortons wasn't too much for the job! All he had to do was start the ball rolling . . . and he meant to do it as soon as he got back to town.

It was late afternoon as Annie and Tagg came back from a gallop up into the hills. All day they had been "hashing over" the party. They agreed that they had had the best time ever. Tagg had eaten all the ice cream he could devour and still stay off the sick list, and he had met some boys his own age who hadn't minded admitting they envied him the excitement of his long trip west. He still had a few yarns in reserve to spring on them the next time they met. Diablo promised to be quite a nice place to live.

Annie had carefully laid away the precious wedding dress in the old trunk again. As she turned the key in the rusty lock, she hadn't been able to keep from wondering when she would get another chance to wear the pretty thing. She was trying hard to put the Shanleys' offer out of her mind, but she couldn't help thinking about it. What kind, generous people they were! At least, Mr. Shanley was. About Edith she wasn't so positive. A couple of times

last night, when she was telling about the trip here, she had
the feeling that Edith was a little bored. And once she
had turned to Edith, suddenly, and caught a black look on
her pretty face. Edith had smiled right away, but Annie
couldn't help remembering the frown. She was sorry, because she wanted very much to like Edith—her father and
Uncle Luke being such good friends.

Tagg was leading the two horses to the barn, as Annie
started toward the house, carrying her rifle. As she walked
around the corner of the house, she saw a man run
from the kitchen yard in the direction of the thicket
beyond the pole corral. For a moment she was too surprised
to do anything, then she called out, "Hey! You!" and
started to run after him. He was a good hundred feet ahead
of her when he disappeared into the thick brush, but she
had had enough of a look at him to recognize Rufe Horton,
the horse thief she had brought to Diablo as a prisoner.

She ran across the yard and plunged into the thicket
after him. She was brought up short by the deafening roar
of a six-shooter, and in the same second, a bullet smashed
into the trunk of a tree not over a foot from her head. She
couldn't see Horton, but he evidently could see her!

She dropped to the ground, flat, and lay there, but her

Springfield was pointed in the direction the shot had come from. If he came to see what luck he had had, she would be ready for him!

But a moment later, she heard a heavy crashing in the brush, and right afterward, the sound of pounding hoofs moving rapidly away.

Outside the barn, Tagg was yelling wildly, "Annie! Sis! Where are you?"

"Here I am!" she called, running up. "Where's Target? Did you get him unsaddled?"

"Not yet! What's going on? What did you shoot at?"

"I didn't shoot. It was that horse thief, Rufe Horton! I saw him coming out of the house, and I ran after him into the thicket. He shot at me but he missed. And then he rode off. I'm going after him!"

Tagg stood puzzling. "What was he doing in the house? Did he steal anything?"

"I haven't looked yet. Maybe we better!"

They raced toward the house. The living room seemed undisturbed, and Annie and Tagg went over the rest of the rooms without noticing anything out of place. If he had come to ransack the place, he must have lost his nerve when he saw her coming up outside with her rifle in hand.

Annie suddenly stopped and studied the braided rug in Uncle Luke's bedroom. Horton had left muddy heel marks all over the room. She knew they weren't Luke's because she had swept the room thoroughly after he left for Diablo that morning. But the bureau drawers were closed, and the sheriff's wardrobe doors were closed tight just as she had shut them when she hung his clean white shirt in it an hour ago. Except for the muddy tracks, the room looked exactly as she had left it.

She felt sure Rufe Horton had come there to steal, but what was he after in Uncle Luke's room?

"I'll get the horses and we'll catch him!" Tagg dashed out the door and was halfway to the barn before he noticed Uncle Luke and Lofty Craig riding in. He changed direction and ran to them, yelling the exciting news about the prowler.

As Annie hurried up with her rifle in hand, Luke was shaking his head at Tagg. "Lofty'll go after him, button. It isn't a job for you and Annie."

Lofty checked his shiny Winchester. "I'll get him." He started toward the back yard.

"At least you might ask what direction he took!" Annie said coldly.

"Just point," Lofty drawled. "I reckon I can pick up the trail."

Annie pointed, with a stabbing forefinger. And Lofty rode quickly toward the thicket. "I hope," she told her uncle stiffly, "that he's as good a trailer as he seems to think!"

Luke got down slowly from his horse and told Tagg, "Put him away, son." Then as Tagg led the big gray off to the barn, Luke explained, "The way things are going, honey, if anybody rounds up that horse thief, it's got to be Lofty or me."

"Has something more happened?" She could see it had.

MacTavish nodded. "Last night, while we were at the party at Shanleys', somebody broke into Ben Crane's office up at the Lucy K. mine, and smashed his new safe to bits. Got his whole month's payroll. Second time it's happened in three months, and Ben is fit to be tied. We just had a big blowup at the jail over it. Ben was yellin' so loud, it brought John Shanley all the way from the land office to see what was the matter." He shook his head. "Honey, if it hadn't been for John, I think I would've handed my star over to Ben Crane right then and there. But John stood up for me and Lofty."

Annie listened, wide-eyed. "I bet he did!"

"Sometimes I get so fed up, Annie, that I wish I had enough money to get away from Diablo and take you kids with me! I'm sick of taking all the blame for everything that happens in the county!" He was still thinking of that letter in his pocket, from the governor. And some of the sarcastic things Ben Crane had said stuck in his mind.

"Uncle Luke," Annie hesitated over it, "I've never met this Mr. Crane, but I was wondering—do you think he might be starting trouble so he can put somebody else in your job? Maybe he's mixed up with those outlaws, and they're just hoping to run things their own way after they get rid of you."

"Ben Crane—with outlaws?" Luke MacTavish was startled. He thought it over, and then shook his head firmly. "No, honey. Ben's ornery and loud-mouthed, and he's on the wrong track right now because he's sore at losing his cash, but I've known Ben for twenty years, and he's as honest as—" he groped for a comparison, "as honest as John Shanley, himself!"

## 12       The Trap Springs

It was the middle of the morning when Dude Rango, in a travel-stained pair of jeans and a clean but worn hickory shirt, came clattering down the middle of Diablo's main street. He was riding a tired brown horse, and leading a burro that was loaded down with an assortment of mining tools. The pick and shovel and the thin sheet-iron pan were trade-marks of the prospector he was impersonating.

John Shanley was conveniently on hand in front of his land office, to greet the stranger with a show of surprise and interest. He hurried him inside, and the door closed quickly after them.

Those who were near at the moment—and there were several citizens with an eye out for news—noticed that the stranger was carrying a small sack which showed suspicious sharp bulges. It must have been quartz samples he brought, they agreed later, but at the moment they were only mildly interested, and wondered what the hurry was all about.

The stranger stayed a long time in Shanley's office, and the gossips soon lost interest and went on about more pressing business. If they had continued to watch, they would have seen Shanley leave his office after a while to go up the street to the jail. And they would have seen him stroll back, very casually, with Sheriff Luke at his side. Both men entered the office, and again the door was closed tight.

Back at the sheriff's office, Lofty Craig gloomily took over. He had had no luck last evening trying to track the fugitive, and he was a little disturbed that John Shanley had been so mysterious when he came to get Sheriff Luke just now. Lofty had been getting quite a few black looks from the local folks lately, because of the jail break, and the robbery at Ben Crane's mine. If he could have caught up with Rufe Horton last night, it would have done a lot for his standing.

Even the waitress over at the hotel didn't bring meals to him any more. She was annoyed with him, and wouldn't even talk to him, since he had been forced to confess that the dinner she had cooked for *him* had been served to Rufe Horton, instead.

On the whole, Lofty was feeling pretty low as he stared out the window onto the hot, dusty street. He wondered what was going on down at the land office. Sheriff Luke would tell him, he felt sure.

But Luke didn't give Lofty any explanations when he returned from that closed-door conference at Shanley's. He seemed excited, but not worried. He was in very good spirits, and joked more than he had for many weeks. But even though Lofty hinted broadly and did everything but come out and ask what was going on, Luke made no effort to explain.

It was just as Luke was locking up the back door of the empty jail and getting ready to close up for the night, that he gave Lofty any kind of a hint as to what had been discussed. "I'm pulling out early in the morning from the ranch," he told Lofty. "I'll leave you in charge."

"You going to the capital?" Lofty asked.

Sheriff Luke smiled and shook his head. "Nope. Headed the other way, as it happens. Got some business to tend to."

"Yeah?" Lofty encouraged him.

"Private business," Sheriff Luke grinned. "Can't tell you right now, but you'll hear all about it in time." And that was all he would say.

Lofty was disturbed. In the two years that he had been deputy, he couldn't remember another time when Sheriff MacTavish had been mysterious about anything. He usually made it a point to tell Lofty exactly where he was going and what it was about.

Lofty agreed rather gloomily to stay on the job and take care of anything that came up. He had an idea that, as usual, his only activity would be to quiet some miner who felt like celebrating.

Sheriff Luke rode off to the ranch in an unusually cheerful mood. He was full of fun all evening, and kept Tagg entertained with all sorts of yarns.

Annie was relieved and happy to see him so relaxed. He seemed to have shaken off the gloomy mood that had held him ever since their arrival. He didn't make any explanation, but he dropped a hint now and then during supper and later as they sat in front of the crackling fire, that he had a very good reason for being cheerful. Annie waited to hear the secret of his changed outlook, but bedtime came and he still made no explanation.

"He's so much like Tagg," she thought affectionately, as she prepared for bed, "with his big secret. I bet he won't be able to keep it through breakfast!"

But it was still long before the usual rising time, when Annie sat up in bed and listened. She was positive that someone was moving around out in the barn. One of the horses was stamping and snorting.

She pulled a heavy flannel wrapper over her long-sleeved nightgown and put on her bedroom slippers. The snorting was still going on out there. She reached for her six-shooter, and in the darkness made sure that it was fully loaded. Then she quietly left the room and made for the kitchen door, pistol in hand.

In the dark kitchen, she was crossing to the door, when she heard a slight sound behind her. She whirled, stepping back against the wall away from the window, so she would not be outlined against the grayness of the early dawn.

"I've got a gun, and it's pointed at you," she said, in a quiet tone. "Whoever you are, better reach for the ceiling!"

"It's me, Annie!" It was a shaky small voice.

She lowered the Colt. "Tagg Oakley, what are you prowling around for this time of night?"

"I heard you go by my room just now," he whispered, coming to her. "Is something wrong?"

"Sounds like it, in the barn," she answered in the same quiet tone. "Keep your voice down so we don't wake up

Uncle Luke. It may be just a rat that's got the horses upset, but I aim to find out."

"Can I come?" Tagg held her sleeve tightly.

"I suppose so," she answered, "but keep back of me, and if I run into that horse thief or any other trouble his size, you scoot back here and wake up Uncle Luke."

"Sure, Annie!" Tagg was delighted at being included in the war party. Annie moved quickly out of the back door, her Colt cocked and ready, and Tagg started after her. He stopped only long enough to pick up the heavy iron poker that stood beside the old fireplace. He had no intention of running away if Annie bumped into trouble. He was going to stand his ground right beside her.

She stopped in the doorway of the big barn and stared in surprise. Uncle Luke was saddling his gray by the light of a shaded oil lantern.

"Uncle Luke!" She lowered the Colt and carefully uncocked it. "I thought you were somebody trying to steal the horses!"

Luke MacTavish looked uncomfortable. "Hi, there, young 'uns!" he said. "Sorry I got you up. I've got an errand to tend to, and I thought I'd get going without waking you." He slapped the gray horse, half playfully. "This fellow thought he'd rather sleep, and kicked up a fuss."

"I'm glad he did," Annie said, "or you'd have started out without a bite of breakfast." She laughed. "And we don't allow that in this high-class boarding house. I'm going right straight in and whip up a batch of flapjacks and a pot of coffee." She turned to go.

"No, wait, honey!" Sheriff Luke spoke hastily. "I don't have time. I've got some bread and cheese in my saddlebags, and a canteen full of our good well water. That's all I need for breakfast this morning."

"What difference will half an hour make?" Annie was a little surprised at her usually hungry uncle.

"I'm meeting a feller up the road a piece," Luke was already leading the gray outside the barn, "and I don't want to keep him waiting."

"Why don't we invite him to eat, too?" Tagg was curious to see who it was.

"No," his uncle brushed it aside, "not this morning. We're in a hurry."

When he was mounted, he looked down at the pair. Annie was standing beside Tagg, her arm over the boy's shoulder, and they were both looking up at him with puzzled curiosity. He frowned. "I know you're bustin' to

know what this is all about," he said gravely, "but you'll
have to wait a bit. You'll hear soon enough, though I can't
say just when. Maybe a day or two, maybe longer. And,
Annie—" he leaned over to touch her shoulder, "when
it comes to trips to Paris and all the rest of it, maybe you'll
be having them, too, before long. Might be some changes
around here for all of us!"

Before either of them could answer, he had started up
the big gray, and was cantering off.

"What was Uncle Luke talking about?" Tagg's small
face was puzzled.

Annie shook her head, unsmiling. "I don't know, button," she said, turning him back toward the house and
keeping her arm protectingly over his shoulder, "but somehow, I'm worried. It isn't like him to be so mysterious."

"Wonder who it is he's meeting," Tagg persisted.

"We'll know—when he gets back and is ready to tell
us. Meantime, let's get ourselves some of those hotcakes
he didn't want. There's a new jug of molasses just aching
to be used."

All through the long morning, Annie battled a feeling
that she couldn't quite put a name to. She felt as if some-

thing were hanging over her, something unpleasant. It was the same sensation she had often had just before a thunder storm, when the whole sky turned a strange yellow and the wind died down and everything was still, very still. Then the thunder would start, very faint at first and far away, then louder and louder; and the lightning flashes would light up the sky, and come closer and closer, till finally the rain would come sweeping down and drench the whole place. When it came there was never any telling how long it would last, or what damage it would do. But there was no way of putting it off, or of stopping it, once it started. And she had the same strange feeling today, that something was going to happen and there was nothing she could do to stop it!

It was still early in the afternoon when she decided to saddle Target and ride into town to talk to Lofty Craig. She was hoping that, without telling him what was worrying her, she could get some reassurance that everything was all right.

Tagg wanted to go with her, but she convinced him that someone should stay there and keep an eye out for Rufe Horton, in case he sneaked back. She made the boy promise not to interfere with the badman, if he did show up, but to

keep out of his way, and then ride after her the moment
Horton left. She felt that they had scared him off earlier,
and he might come back a second time for whatever he was
looking for. She was careful to leave her uncle's bedroom
in perfect order, so they would know if anything had been
disturbed.

Tagg was excited at being entrusted with an important
job like this. He took up his post in the comfortable crotch
of the big cottonwood tree that stood in the front yard.
From his perch there, he could see in all directions around
the ranch house. He was well fortified with thick slices of
Annie's fresh homemade bread, slathered with butter right
out of the churn, and two pocketfuls of gingersnaps, the
"store-boughten" kind that were his favorite.

Annie waved back as she started Target through the gate,
though she couldn't see Tagg up in the tree. Then she
gave the horse free rein and headed for Diablo.

She felt that all she needed, to put her mind at ease, was
a few words with Lofty. She was quite certain that Luke
must have given his deputy a great deal more information
about his trip away from Diablo than he had offered her.

But Lofty, who was still nursing hurt feelings over being
shut out of Luke's confidence, was sulky and not inclined

to unbend. He neither admitted that he knew where her uncle had gone, nor that he didn't.

She was leaving the sheriff's office when she heard three shots in rapid succession. It was the old pioneer signal for help, the one she had used outside the Smoke Tree Station when she and Tagg were in danger of being shut out. Somebody was in trouble.

Half the town was in the street waiting by the time the fast-galloping rider had pulled to a stop in the middle of the street, swayed a moment in his saddle, then tumbled off into the dust, apparently unconscious.

Annie got to him first, and saw that the man was a stranger to her. His left sleeve was caked with blood, and his shirt clung wetly to him as if he had been riding hard and long. The horse, panting hard, stood drooping and exhausted.

By the time others had run up, Annie had made a quick inspection of his arm and seen that it was only a slight flesh wound. She suggested that they carry the wounded man into the sheriff's office and call Doc Busby. But as they started to lift him, he sat up and pushed them away, staring around wildly.

"Shanley!" he croaked. "Bring John Shanley here!"

The storekeeper ran down the street yelling for Shanley, who promptly appeared in his doorway and came running with his long coattails flying out behind him.

The stranger was on his feet, swaying and clutching his arm, as Shanley came up.

Shanley took one look at his face. "Good heavens, Mr. Rango!" He grabbed the wounded man by his good arm. "Speak up, man! What happened? Where's Luke Mac-Tavish?"

Rango seemed on the verge of collapse as he answered between groans, but loud enough for everyone within a radius of ten feet to hear: "MacTavish shot . . . me. . . ."

"Luke shot you?" John Shanley almost shouted the words. He shook Rango roughly. "Why? What are you saying?"

Rango steadied himself on his feet and faced Shanley. Out of the corner of his eye, he saw Annie and Lofty, both of them suspicious and alert. He had better make a convincing story out of this. He paused dramatically. Then, with a very good imitation of anger, he told Shanley, loudly: "He tricked you, Shanley—he had his gang ambush us halfway to Jumpoff! He got away with every cent of your money! And he tried to kill me!"

## 13            Rango's Story

Rango's accusation against the sheriff started a wild clamor of excitement in the crowd. John Shanley did his best to look shocked and horrified. "My money—gone!" He repeated it several times, as if he couldn't believe it.

Big Ben Crane, striding up to see what was causing the excited yelling, roared angrily when he found out. "I knew it! I've been warning you there was something crooked going on right under your noses!" He yelled at Lofty: "Don't stand around, Craig! Get up a posse!"

Shanley stole a quick look at Annie. She wore a look of stunned amazement. He spoke quickly for her benefit: "No! Wait! We haven't heard the whole story yet. Maybe there's some mistake!" He turned to Rango. "Go on!"

"There's no mistake, Mr. Shanley," Rango snapped. "We'd gone about six miles on the old Jumpoff trail, when a bullet smacked into a rock in front of my horse. It came from across the canyon.

"I pulled up quick. There was no place to hide, but I yelled to MacTavish to wheel and head back. I could see somebody hiding in the rocks across the canyon. Couldn't tell if there was more than one, and I couldn't take a chance on a gun fight, carrying your money."

Someone in the crowd spoke: "Money?"

John Shanley nodded, frowning. "He and MacTavish were on a private errand for me," he explained hastily. "What happened next?" he barked at Rango. "Get to the point, man!"

"I'm doing the best I can," Rango groaned, nursing his wounded arm.

Lofty brought him a drink of water, and after a moment, Rango was able to go on. "Instead of turning, like I expected, MacTavish pulled his gun and shot at me, point blank. My horse was moving, and it only got me in the arm. I reared my horse and drove at him. He ducked and clubbed me with the gun. That's all I remember till I woke up, stretched out in the trail, and the money gone."

"How much did he get away with?" Ben Crane was openly curious.

Rango let Shanley answer. The land agent's voice shook with pretended indignation as he told Crane, loudly enough for everyone to hear, "Twenty thousand dollars in gold and currency—just about every cent I had in the bank!"

"Twenty thousand!" It was Crane again. The big man's voice boomed out, "What kind of an errand did you send that much money on? Why didn't you send a draft?"

"It had to be cash. Mr. Rango brought me a land deal that looked worth the chance." John Shanley sank down on the jail steps, fanning himself with his stovepipe hat and looking dejected. The crowd muttered sympathetically, more than one stealing a glance at Annie to see how she was taking this.

She stood silent, her face white and drawn, looking from Rango to John Shanley.

"I can't explain, folks, because it was a private deal," Shanley went on, "just between Mr. Rango and me."

"How did Luke get in on it, if it was so private?" It was the shrewd little owner of the general store, an old friend of the sheriff's. He was curious about the deal, and he was suspicious of the glib-tongued Rango on general principles.

Annie noticed that several of the other men felt the same

way, and she was heartened at the evidence that all Diablo wasn't ready to condemn her uncle on a stranger's wild story.

"That," said Rango, "was his own idea. And we were fools enough to let him put it over."

Shanley explained, "You see, when Mr. Rango and I agreed to go into this business deal, I was a little worried about sending that much cash without somebody to guard it. So I suggested to Mr. Rango that we get Luke MacTavish to suggest a reliable man to ride along with Mr. Rango as a bodyguard. He was agreeable, and I brought Luke over to my office to talk about it. I was a bit surprised when he said he'd take on the job himself."

"I was, too," Rango chimed in, "but he was pretty smooth about it. He said nobody'd think anything about him riding out early in the morning that way, because they'd think he was trailing that horse thief that got out of jail so easy."

"Yeah, some people might have thought so." Ben Crane cast a hard look at Lofty, who hadn't gotten over the shock of Rango's accusation and was standing silent and unhappy beside Annie. "But the rest of us have got our own ideas on how that horse thief was let go—and *why!*"

"Let go?" Lofty roared. "That does it!" He lashed out

with his fist at Ben Crane. The older man was his equal in
size, and a tough fighter. Lofty's fist clipped him on the chin
and staggered him for a second. Then, with an angry bel-
low, he waded in with both fists flying.

The crowd, delighted at any kind of a fight, gave way
for the two men to battle in the middle of the street.

Annie watched in worried silence, as first one and then
the other landed a blow. Fighting never settled anything,
she thought, and wished unhappily that they would stop it.

Rango and John Shanley watched in baffled anger, as
Lofty toppled Ben Crane with a wild rush and the crowd
roared gleefully and cheered the deputy. The two schemers
exchanged quick glances. The fight was distracting Diablo's
attention from the robbery story. And Lofty Craig was win-
ning the crowd's approval at a time when Shanley wanted
it to turn against both Luke and Lofty.

Shanley stepped quickly toward the fighters, who were
rolling in the middle of the street, punching at each other.
"Stop it!" he yelled. "Stop!"

There was an angry growl of protest from the men who
lined the wooden sidewalk. They resented Shanley's inter-
ference. But Shanley grabbed Lofty by the arm and tried
to jerk him to his feet as the deputy was lifting his doubled

fist to land a blow on Crane's jaw. An annoyed bystander on the sidewalk grabbed up a thick chunk of wood and aimed it at the back of Shanley's head.

Annie saw the chunk starting to fly through the air. She jerked her gun from its holster and took split-second aim. Her bullet caught the heavy missile in mid-air and smashed it into splinters.

The roar of the six-shooter put a quick end to the fight. Both Lofty and Ben Crane scrambled to their feet, grimy and exhausted, and looked around wildly, both reaching for their guns in a natural reaction to the shot. John Shanley had wheeled, his own hand going to the shoulder holster inside his long coat. His hand dropped quickly to his side, as he saw Annie, smoking Colt in hand, grinning at him.

The man who had flung the chunk of wood pushed his way hurriedly back into the crowd and disappeared before he could be grabbed. There were half a dozen who had seen what had happened, and they all tried to tell it at once, and to congratulate Annie on her quickness and skill with the six-shooter.

"Good thing she saw him in time," one of them said.

"Ma'am," said another, "you sure can handle that there weepun of yours!"

And Shanley, with a great show of gratitude, thanked her and assured her that he wouldn't forget her alertness.

"It seems as if I'm always having to say 'thank you' to you, Annie."

"It wasn't anything," she answered soberly. "I just happened to see him in time. What are you going to do—" she swallowed hard, "about Uncle Luke?"

"I'm afraid there's nothing we can do," he kept a note of regret in his voice, "except to send a posse out to look for him and his gang."

"I still think—I mean I just *know* there must be some mistake!" Her eyes were brimming and she turned her head away so that Shanley wouldn't see her tears. "I can't believe Uncle Luke'd do anything wrong!"

"It's hard for me to believe, too," he shook his head, sadly, "but I'm afraid the temptation was too much for him. Twenty thousand dollars is a lot of money, Annie. And we don't know how deeply he's involved with those outlaws. Maybe Luke wants to be honest, but he's in too far."

Annie was silent. She was still not convinced. There was nothing crooked about the man she and Tagg had grown to love in the few days they had been here. And nobody could make her think so.

Shanley saw how she felt. He decided to build it up a little more. "There's more to it than just the story Rango told. When Luke offered to ride along with Rango and guard that money, he let slip to us that he was in a very bad way for money himself. I don't know what was going on. It sounded to me as if somebody might be blackmailing him. Naturally, I couldn't ask questions."

"If you thought that, why did you let him go? Weren't you afraid he'd take your money, after all the things people like Mr. Crane have said about him?"

"No. He gave me a good reason for wanting to get to Jumpoff."

Annie's eyes were stormy. Shanley spoke quickly: "I'm going to tell you something I don't want anyone else in Diablo to know."

"I won't say anything to anyone, Mr. Shanley."

"I believe you, Annie. First, let me tell you that it wasn't a land deal Mr. Rango brought me. There's been a gold strike at Jumpoff, and it's still a secret, even to most people up there. Rango gave me a chance to get in on it with him, for that twenty thousand dollars."

Her eyes widened. He could see she believed him. Shanley went on briskly. "We hadn't intended to tell Luke what

was in the air, but something slipped out, and right away
he offered to ride along with Rango, so that he could get in
on the strike. He said he had some money owed to him at
Jumpoff, and if he could get his hands on it, he wanted to
invest in a claim for you kids, up there. I believed it. It never
occurred to me he was planning to rob Rango and me, and
not go anywhere near the gold strike!"

He watched Annie narrowly, and saw that she was uncertain and worried now. He had told her a good, believable
story, and it had had its effect.

He shook his head sadly. "Well, what's done is done,
and there's nothing we can do now but try to find him, and
bring him back." Then he added, sternly, "In the meantime, we must keep Mr. Rango's secret about the gold strike.
Don't mention it to anyone, or you'll start a stampede to
Jumpoff, and it wouldn't be fair to Rango. He must have
his chance to find other financing, now that I can no longer
spare any money to invest."

Annie promised soberly not to tell anyone, even Tagg.
She felt miserable to think that Shanley had lost not only
his twenty thousand dollars, but also his chance to make
many times that much buying and selling the claims.

Lofty and Ben Crane were still growling at each other,

as the posse of five men was being organized. Crane was openly against letting Lofty go with the posse. "He's MacTavish's deputy," he declared, "and his friend. How do we know he won't destroy any trail MacTavish has left, and keep us from tracking him down?"

Lofty, on his part, loudly refused to believe any part of the story told by the stranger, Rango. He declared that when the truth came out, it would be discovered that it was all a plot to discredit, and possibly kill, the innocent sheriff, and that Ben Crane would be found to be mixed up in it somewhere!

Lofty's theory was hooted at by some, and mildly supported by others. But there was a general feeling of "wait and see" around Diablo, with an undercurrent of curiosity as to what the twenty thousand dollars had been meant for, and an equally strong undercurrent of sympathy for Annie Oakley and her little brother, who had come a long way only to get a crushing blow like this.

Doc Busby finished bandaging the slight wound in Rango's arm, and pronounced it the least scratch he had ever worked on. He peered over his glasses at the sharp-featured young patient and pulled at his mustache thoughtfully. "Always thought Luke MacTavish was a better shot than that. Seems funny he missed at such close range."

Rango glared at him. "Meaning you wish he hadn't, hey, sawbones? Too bad to disappoint you!" And he stalked over to where Annie and John Shanley stood apart.

Doc Busby looked over his specs after the rangy gunman and shook his head. "Tch! tch!" he told himself, "that is a nasty-tempered man, Busby. I don't think I like him."

Rango strode up to Shanley and Annie. "Looks like we got our posse. You going along, Mr. Shanley?"

"I hadn't planned to," Shanley answered.

"I'm going," Annie turned to hurry toward Target.

"Uh-uh!" Rango disagreed abruptly. She stopped and looked coldly at him. "We'll be moving too fast to bother with taking a girl along."

Annie's eyes flashed. "You don't have much to say about it, Mr. Rango. It's my uncle you're looking for, and I aim to be close by when you find him. It's a good story you tell about what happened to Mr. Shanley's money, but that doesn't mean it's true. Twenty thousand dollars could have looked just as big to you as you claim it did to my uncle."

Rango glared. "If you weren't only a puny female—" he

doubled his fist suggestively. Annie smiled her contempt and held her ground. Lofty had already started over to see what was going on, when Rango's fist dropped to his side, and he turned away abruptly.

"Better get started," Shanley advised hastily. Rango stalked to his horse and hauled it around roughly as he mounted. Annie watched him with a frown. When she turned to Shanley, he shook his head regretfully. "I suppose if you want to ride along with the posse, Annie, it'll be all right, but some of the outlaws might still be around."

"I'll have to see them before I believe Mr. Rango's story," she retorted, and ran to mount her cow pony.

Shanley was worried. He had had no chance to talk to Rango privately, to find out what had really happened out at the ambush. Now the posse would be snooping around out there, and unless Rango had been careful to destroy any evidence against his story, Annie's sharp eyes might turn up something to betray him.

He decided suddenly that he would ride along with the posse. If Annie got suspicious, he might be able to talk her out of it—somehow.

"Wait!" he called, hurrying toward the group of riders as they got ready to move up the street. "I'll go with you!"

# 14                               A Discovery

It was hot and dusty along the steep hill trail that led to distant Jumpoff. The posse rode slowly and with much complaint. It was a long ride, and, they argued among themselves, if MacTavish and his gang had stolen the money, as the stranger claimed, they would be long gone from the ambush spot by now! Just the same, the posse kept their guns ready and their eyes alert as they rode.

Rango kept in the lead, and Lofty and Ben Crane followed him closely. Shanley would have liked to catch up with Rango and find out privately what had really happened at the ambush, but he didn't get a chance. He would have to wait.

Annie rode in silence, unhappy and confused over the situation. She knew that some of the men accepted Rango's story without question, but some of them did not. They had

known Uncle Luke too long to believe the word of a
stranger.

Annie was hoping hard that Rango's story hadn't been
true. Maybe, she admitted, there had been some kind of
an outlaw attack, just as he claimed. And maybe Uncle
Luke *had* shot at Rango. But if so, Luke must have been
hurt or confused, and hadn't realized what he was doing.
But that opened another frightening possibility—maybe
the outlaws had hurt Uncle Luke badly and they would
find him out here, wounded or—she refused to say the
frightening word, even in her thoughts. She was worried
sick, and wished they could travel faster, but the trail was
steep and dangerous, and they had to plod along.

Up ahead, Rango pulled up and signaled for a halt. The
trail was narrow and overgrown here, and the tracks,
which Annie had been studying all the way, were suddenly
lost in the hoofprints of other horses. The dirt was kicked
up, as if a struggle had taken place.

"This is the place," Rango called out.

Annie pulled toward the edge and looked over. There
was a sheer drop of many feet to where the tops of trees
made a solid, concealing mass. Target's foot kicked a small
boulder; she could hear it bounding down for what seemed

half a minute. She drew back from the edge, and guided
the nervous cow pony ahead to join Rango and Lofty.

Rango pointed across the deep canyon toward a big outcrop of rocks, jumbled together on the steep hillside.
"That's where his gang were hiding when they took the
shot at me and missed me!" he announced.

The posse studied the rocks across the way. There was no
evidence of life there now. No sunlight glittered on rifle
barrels. The posse breathed easier, to a man.

"Where's the rock over here that you said the bullet
smacked into?" Annie challenged Rango. "It should be
around here somewhere—if you didn't imagine it."

Rango looked at her with cordial dislike, and moved
ahead slowly, searching the rocks that lined the wall of
the trail. Shanley followed, pushing past the others and
pretending to help him hunt.

"I hope you didn't lie about that shot," he whispered;
"she doesn't believe you."

Annie's keen eyes scanned the rocky wall beside the trail.
Lofty, tall in the saddle, was the first to spot the splash of
lead on the granite, up high. He stood in his stirrups and
moved a mesquite bush out of the way to show it to Annie.

Her heart sank. Rango's story about someone shooting

from across the canyon was true. She could tell by the narrow area in which the bullet had spattered, that it had come a considerable distance. And the angle at which it had chipped off slivers of granite proved that it had actually been fired from somewhere near that rocky outcrop across the way, just as he had told them.

Her eyes met Rango's. He was smiling coldly. "Well?" he asked.

Annie nodded and turned away. She was too worried to be able to give him an answer just then. Lofty dug out the spent bullet and dropped it in his pocket.

Rango dismounted and picked up a second lead slug from the dirt. He handed it to Lofty with a mocking smile. "Here, take this one, too. It oughta fit your crooked sheriff's gun. It's probably the one he nicked me with."

Annie began to ride ahead slowly, studying the ground closely as she went. Shanley and Rango exchanged uneasy glances as she wheeled suddenly and cantered back. She wore a puzzled look as she spoke to Shanley, ignoring Rango.

"My uncle's horse had one crooked shoe," she told Shanley. "All the way here, I've been able to pick up his trail by that track. But there's no sign of it beyond here."

"So?" Rango shrugged it off. "Maybe his gang brought him a fresh horse, because his was lame—or tired."

"There's no sign that Uncle's gray was lame! And he's often ridden it thirty miles in a day," she insisted, "so why would it be tired after going less than five?"

"I'll ask him when we catch him!" Rango said angrily. "How does anybody know why a man changes horses? Maybe the gray was saddlesore—or the other horse was faster."

Rango turned away abruptly, to the other members of the posse. "I guess we'd just be wasting your time, gents, trying to track an old fox like MacTavish. By now he's well on his way to the border."

John Shanley shook his head. "Looks like it, Rango. But Lofty here can wire his description to every town within fifty miles and warn them to be on the lookout for him. I hate to go on record against a man I've always thought so much of, but I guess it's up to me, as the heavy loser, to offer a reward for him." He turned to Lofty with a sigh. "Better make it five hundred, Deputy. Dead or alive."

Annie gave a horrified exclamation. "No, please!"

Rango spoke harshly. "Why not? Are you still stupid enough to think I'm lying?"

"I don't know if I'm stupid or not. But I know my Uncle Luke. He *couldn't* be a thief and a leader of a gang of outlaws. I don't care what *you* say."

"Agh!" Rango waved her aside. "Women!"

Ben Crane spoke for the first time. His voice was gentler than usual as he addressed Annie. "I've known Luke a lot longer than anybody else in this bunch, Annie—and there was a time when I thought I knew him mighty well. But men change, and it looks like your uncle's changed along with many another. It's the gold fever does it. And we can all understand it, even if we want to see justice done to any lawbreakers, no matter who they are."

"But there's no evidence against Uncle Luke—only this man's word—this stranger!" Annie's voice was desperate.

"Mr. Rango is no stranger to *me*," John Shanley said sternly; "he is a reputable citizen of Jumpoff. And I must take his word as to what happened, because there is no evidence to contradict it."

"Now, wait!" Rango glared at Annie. "I don't like you calling me a liar, Miss Know-it-all! From what I hear around Diablo, your uncle has been pretty slack about enforcing the law. And I'll lay a bet if we took a good look around that Bull's-Eye ranch of his, we'd find plenty of signs that this isn't his first robbery!"

Annie flared angrily. "Why don't you—every one of you —come along right now and look? You won't find anything, because there's nothing to find!"

"Now, Miss Annie," Ben Crane tried to soothe her. "That won't be necessary a-tall." He frowned at Rango.

"Sounds like a good idea to me!" Rango winked at John Shanley, unnoticed by the others.

"Come on!" Annie headed Target back toward Diablo. "And you better keep up with me," she flung at Rango, "so you can be sure I don't destroy any 'evidence'!"

"If that's the way she feels about it, let's go!" Ben Crane advised them. "Me, I'm still sittin' on the fence and I'm waitin' to see which way to jump."

Annie kept up a fast pace all the way to the ranch. She was so sure that they would find nothing to prove Uncle Luke had done anything wrong, that she could hardly wait to get there with the posse. The men had to push their horses to keep up with the fleet-footed Target.

Lofty rode close to Rango all the way, and the disgusted outlaw had no chance to talk to John Shanley in private. Shanley tried a couple of times to speed up and get alongside Rango. He wanted very much to know what had really happened out here. But each time he tried, Lofty was within hearing distance.

Tagg was still perched up in the cottonwood lookout post, as the riders swept into view along the ranch road. He had been curled up in the crotch of the tree, half asleep, when the pounding of hoofs brought him suddenly awake.

He peered out, expecting to see Rufe Horton and at least one other outlaw. Instead, he saw Annie riding at the head of more than half a dozen men. He dropped out of the tree as she rode into the yard, with Lofty and the rest of the riders close behind her. "Hi, Annie!" he yelled.

She pulled to a sliding stop. "Hi, ya!" she called, but her usual flashing smile was absent. She looked tired and worried as she swung to the ground. "Lofty, you can show them in," she told the deputy.

Lofty nodded gloomily and started for the front door. He was still convinced that Ben Crane was back of the whole thing, and he was afraid that something had happened to Luke, no matter what anybody said. He had made up his mind that as soon as these men got through looking for something here that they would never find, he would have a long talk with John Shanley and see what he thought about Ben Crane.

Annie threw the reins over Target's head and let them trail on the ground. The posse was waiting uneasily. She waved her hand toward the house. "Help yourselves, gentlemen," she called. "Start anywhere you like, and don't miss anything!"

Ben Crane looked sheepish, and fussed over his saddle, but he made no move toward the door. The other men of the posse filed up onto the porch. John Shanley came and stood beside Annie. She smiled soberly at him.

"Please go in with them, Mr. Shanley. Then I'll be sure nobody has a chance to lie about finding something. At least, I'll have one witness I can trust!"

Rango stopped a couple of feet away. "Spunky, ain't you?" he drawled. "Too bad it's wasted!"

Annie turned her shoulder to him. At the front door, Lofty was making the posse men wipe the dust off their shoes before he would let them go inside his boss's house.

"What are they looking for, Annie?" Tagg was puzzled.

"They don't know," Annie answered drily, "but they won't find anything in there that shouldn't be in honest folks' houses."

"Annie, I forgot to tell you, Rufe Horton didn't show up," Tagg reported. "I watched real hard for him."

Rango threw a quick side look at Shanley, who kept his face expressionless. Loudly, so that Ben Crane couldn't miss hearing, Rango repeated, "Rufe Horton? Isn't that the horse thief your uncle let out of jail?"

"The one that escaped!" Annie corrected him angrily.

"Annie was afraid he'd come back again, so I was keeping watch for him, like a sentry," Tagg explained proudly.

Ben Crane strode over, scowling. He towered over Tagg. "How often has Horton been here, sonny?"

"We only saw him once. That is, Annie did. I didn't. She scared him off!" He looked at his big sister. "Didn't you, Sis?"

She nodded soberly. She could see suspicion in Ben Crane's face. Crane's eyes met Shanley's. Shanley managed to look bewildered and worried. He had a hard time keeping the triumph that he felt, out of his eyes. He knew what Crane was thinking now—that this proved that the ranch was a hangout for the outlaws! It was all working out much better than Shanley had dared to hope!

"We'd better go in and see that they don't upset the whole house," Shanley spoke briskly. It was better to let Crane think it over, without trying to add anything to that neatly planted suspicion.

He led the way, holding Annie's arm. Tagg and the scowling Ben Crane followed.

Rango watched them, smiling. There was no reason for him to go inside. He knew what they would find.

The men had begun the search in the big, cool living room. They were nervous and awkward. They didn't know just what it was they were looking for, and they didn't know where to start.

Lofty stood off, thumbs hooked in his belt, glaring at them defiantly.

A bit sheepishly, the men made a hurried search of the ceiling-high old desk, and one of them even looked vaguely into the woodbox beside the fireplace. He wasn't sure what he expected to find there, but it seemed a good place to look. Sawdust, splinters, and spiders were the best he could turn up.

"What's this room?" One of the men pointed a thumb toward Annie's door.

"That's Sis's room!" Tagg stood in front of the door with his fists doubled. "And you better keep your noses out of there!"

"Hush, Tagg! Go ahead and look," Annie told the man cheerfully. But he backed off in embarrassed haste, and the door stayed shut. He followed Ben Crane and John Shanley into Sheriff Luke's room.

Annie pulled Tagg to her, and put an arm over his shoulders. "Don't get upset, honey," she told him. "They think they're doing their duty. Let 'em look. There's nothing to hurt Uncle Luke in *this* house!"

Lofty spoke angrily from beside the fireplace. "It's a good thing there's enough of them looking, so they can keep tabs on each other. I don't trust any of 'em, and I've got an idea who could stand the most watching, that Ben Crane—"

There was a sudden excited exclamation from Luke's room. "Here! Look here in the wardrobe!" It was Ben's booming voice. "Look what was hid back of his clothes!"

"Why, it's an empty canvas sack from the Bonanza City Bank!" That was John Shanley's voice.

Then Crane roared, "That's the one my payroll money was in! Look! My bank slip's still inside of it!"

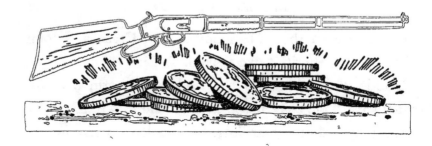

## 15                          Strong Evidence

Lofty and Annie reached Luke MacTavish's room at the same moment, but Tagg was close on their heels.

Ben Crane was holding up a canvas sack with the words BANK OF BONANZA CITY stenciled on it. The sack was empty. In his other hand, he held a bank slip that read: *Lucy K. Mining Co. Account (July Payroll) 100-10's, 50-20's, 500-5's.* Part of a torn five-dollar bill was still clipped to it, as if the thief had ripped it off in careless haste.

Ben let Annie take it and study it. She passed it on to Shanley without a word. Shanley glanced at it with a frown. "I guess we don't need any more evidence than this, Annie. I'm sorry."

She turned away, trying to keep her chin high. Suddenly, Tagg was pulling at her sleeve. "Annie! *I* know! *I* know!"

"What, punkins?" she answered absently.

"I bet I know how that sack got hid inside Uncle Luke's wardrobe!" He was excited, and grinning at them all.

Ben Crane frowned. He was in no mood for playing guessing games. "What's that, Tagg?" he asked impatiently.

"The horse thief put it there!" He turned to Annie. "Don't you remember, we saw his muddy footprints on the carpet in here?"

"That's right!" Annie was excited now. "He was coming from the back of the house when I saw him and chased him. We were afraid he'd stolen something, so we looked in every room to see what was missing. But he hadn't touched a thing anywhere, so far as we could see. Then we came into this room, and saw where he'd left muddy boot prints."

"Why couldn't they have been left by your uncle?" one of the posse men asked.

"Because I swept and dusted the whole house after he rode away this morning!"

"And I helped her!" Tagg boasted.

"Tagg!" Annie gave him a reproving look.

"Well," he amended it, "I did—a little." He saw the

look still in her eye, and added hastily, "That is, I would've, if she'd asked me."

"That's better!" Annie nodded soberly. "We don't have to tell fibs, Tagg. The truth fits better every time." She turned to the men again. "I'm positive that Horton hid that sack here this morning, so Uncle would be blamed when it was found. I don't know who put him up to it, of course." She looked directly at Rango, who had come in as far as the doorway and was lazily draped there, taking it all in.

John Shanley turned away, shaking his head, and Ben Crane's strong jaw stuck out at a stubborn angle.

"There's no use you two trying to cover up for Luke," Ben said impatiently. "This sack is proof enough for me. As for Horton coming here, it looks to me like he's had the run of the place, without you knowing it. You just happened to see him today." He turned to Lofty. "Craig, I'm swearing out a warrant for Luke MacTavish, on the charge of grand theft of my mine payroll."

"And I'm adding attempted murder," Rango chimed in. "What about *you*, Shanley?"

"I've already said I'll offer five hundred dollars reward for him. Better get out the posters at once, Craig, and see that they are mailed to the border towns as soon as possible. I have a feeling that's where he's headed."

Lofty nodded glumly and followed the other men of the posse as they filed silently from the bedroom. Ben Crane stalked after him, but John Shanley sat down heavily in Luke's favorite big chair.

"What are you two going to do now?" he asked Annie, with the most fatherly voice he could manage.

Annie shook her head. "I haven't thought much about it so far, Mr. Shanley. I guess we'll just stay on here for a while and see what happens."

"Do you think that's wise, my dear?"

"I don't know. I haven't had time to decide anything yet. I—I'm sort of confused."

"Then let me help you, child. Let's look at it from all angles." He laid his arm over Tagg's shoulders as he spoke, and drew the boy to him. "The two of you—alone here— might be in real danger. The horse thief that Lofty let escape is probably just one of a gang. Your uncle's gang, it seems now." He shook his head sadly.

"I'll never believe that," Annie put her chin up.

"Of course you don't want to," Shanley went on smoothly. "I don't, either. But the hard facts are there.

Luke is gone—and twenty thousand dollars of my money is gone with him."

"I don't believe Mr. Rango!" Annie was near tears. "No matter what he says! I think he's tricking you!"

"Now, wait, my dear. Since Mr. Rango stood to make a hundred thousand dollars at least from my investment in those claims, why should he steal my twenty thousand?"

"I don't know—all I know is I don't trust him!"

"That's natural, I suppose. But it isn't fair. You don't know anything against Mr. Rango, now do you?"

"No—not actually, of course—but—" she left it unfinished, with a helpless little gesture. "What do you think we ought to do, Tagg and I?"

"I don't think you should stay here," he said. "As a matter of fact, I have plenty of room at my place for both of you, and I know Edith will be delighted to have you there as our guests."

"That's very kind of you," Annie was deeply touched by his generosity, "seeing that Uncle Luke—I mean, seeing that it *looks* like Uncle Luke has stolen all that money from you."

"My dear, you and Tagg are still my very good friends, no matter what trouble Luke has gotten himself into. And

I'm being selfish about asking you to stay at the house with Edith and me, because I know I'd worry if you two were alone out here, with that gang of outlaws on the loose. If they've been making this ranch their headquarters, the way it looks now, then you might both be in real danger any day or night from them."

"Horton's the only stranger we've ever seen here," Annie insisted.

John Shanley shrugged. "So far, maybe. But that doesn't mean they haven't been here! I'd sleep easier at night if I knew you were safe under my roof."

"I don't figure they'd bother me much," Annie said, very quietly. "I'm able to take care of myself 'most anywhere. But the button here, that's different. I wouldn't want him to run up against the Horton kind some time when I wasn't on hand."

"Then I can count on your coming to stay at our place?"

Annie hesitated only a moment more. Tagg looked very small and helpless in the shelter of John Shanley's arm. She nodded. "I guess it would be the best thing to do. And thank you, Mr. Shanley. We're proud to have a friend like you."

Shanley smiled modestly. He looked down at Tagg's

tousled head, so she wouldn't see the triumph he knew must show in his eyes. "My dear child, I'm only sorry this terrible thing has happened to hurt you. Edith and I will do our best to make you feel at home with us."

Annie and Tagg watched John Shanley ride off with Lofty and the others. "He's a fine man, Tagg," she told him, "and I hope Edith doesn't mind us being around."

"Golly, why should she? I'll help make ice cream every day if she wants me to!"

Annie laughed. "Six for her and a half dozen for Tagg!" Then she sobered. "Come on, let's get a few clothes together, and lock up the house. It's getting dark, and I do feel a little spooky here now."

"How long do you think we'll stay at Mr. Shanley's?"

"Till they find where Uncle Luke went, and bring him back, I reckon," she said, with a sigh. "Let's get going."

In the big house on the edge of Diablo, John Shanley went directly to his daughter's room. As usual, Edith was primping, for want of anything more exciting to do. She was standing before the long mirror and admiring herself with the aid of a hand glass. He stood in the doorway a moment, watching and deciding on the best way to break the news to her.

"Charming, as usual," he said lightly. "What is this? Another new gown? You'll have me in the poorhouse soon!"

Edith pouted. "This old thing new? It's ready for the rag bag."

"It's very nice just the same—on my beautiful little girl." Shanley smiled as he lighted one of his special cigars and lowered himself gingerly into one of her fragile satin-covered chairs.

Edith's shrewd eyes narrowed. She left the mirror and came over to face him, her arms folded. "All right, Papa. You can save the pretty speeches. What do you think you're going to talk me into this time?"

"Now, honey, don't fly off like that! I just thought you'd like to hear all the latest news of Diablo! It's most amusing!"

"The only news about Diablo that would amuse *me*, would be to hear it had burned down to the ground!" Edith snapped.

"That might happen some day," he laughed. "But listen to this, my dear. The honest sheriff has disappeared with a sackful of my money, and it seems certain that he has been heading an outlaw gang for a long time."

"*Your* money!" Edith exclaimed. "And you're laughing about it!"

"It's an optical illusion, as the magicians say, dear child. There really wasn't any money—and he didn't steal it— and he really *was* quite an honest, but stupid and stubborn man. Outside of those details, it's true."

Edith stamped her foot and her eyes flashed angrily. "Oh, Papa! You know how I hate riddles! Speak plain English."

"Very well, my dear." Shanley spoke drily. "Sheriff Mac-Tavish has disappeared, under suspicious circumstances. And there is a warrant being issued for him, on charges of robbery and attempted murder."

"Which he didn't do, I gather!"

"Of course not."

"Well, I'm glad you're rid of him. Now I won't have to hang around this horrid place any longer, nor be nice to that upstart Annie Oakley. Ugh!" She made a face.

"I'm afraid you will, for a while, my dear! I've invited Annie and Tagg to stay here."

"Why?" Her pretty face was dark with anger. "You know I can't stand her!"

"I don't like her any better than you do. But I have to

keep a close eye on her, till I get that ranch in my name. We must make her think that we're the best friends she has, so that when I offer to help her by taking that old run-down Bull's-Eye ranch off her hands, she'll agree to let me have it at once."

"When will that be? I don't think I can put up with those two very long."

"Maybe a week, maybe two. Just as soon as it's well established that Luke was a crook. Meantime, watch yourself with both of them. Make them feel that they're practically members of the family. Don't say too much about the ranch. It isn't hers yet."

"Then MacTavish didn't get that chance to deed the ranch to her?" She looked admiringly at her father.

John Shanley smiled. "Rango and I moved too fast, but Annie and Tagg are his legal heirs."

"Where *is* the sheriff? I mean—what happened to him, actually?"

"Rango hasn't had time to give me all the details, yet, but he's coming to supper. And I'll hear all about what happened at the ambush—after our little friends are tucked in bed."

"Let's hope he did a good job of it." Edith was applying

a cloud of rice powder to her pretty little nose.

"Don't worry. MacTavish won't bother us again. Just do your part with them." He rose and stepped quickly to the window at the sound of riders on the graveled path. "Ah! Here are our dear young guests now. We must go give them a hearty welcome to their new home!"

Any doubts Annie might have brought with her about how Edith would take their visit were immediately set at rest by Edith's warm greeting. The pretty girl slipped her arm around Annie's waist as she led her and Tagg to their rooms in the west wing.

"I'm so glad you're here," she confided. "You don't know how lonesome this big place gets, with nobody around but the help. Papa is always so busy at the office or out selling land to settlers! We're going to have a wonderful time together!"

"You're right nice to have us here," Annie said soberly. "I just hope we don't put you out too much."

"I can teach you how to ride, if you don't know!" Tagg made himself heard. The two girls seemed to be forgetting that he was around.

"I'd love that!" Edith gave him her prettiest smile. "Only I don't have anything to wear horseback riding. All my clothes are so silly and frilly! But you and I will go shopping for an outfit exactly like you have on," she told Annie gaily. "Then we'll look just like sisters! It'll be such fun!"

She flitted around the big room that was to be Annie's, rolling up the shades and letting the last rays of sunlight through the heavy lace curtains.

"I hope you like this room!" she giggled. "It's the one we call the violet bedroom. See, the wallpaper is all bunches of violets! Papa had it sent out all the way from Philadelphia. And look at the scarf on the mantelpiece—more violets!" She wrinkled her pretty brow suddenly. "Oh, I hope you *like* violets!"

"They're my favorite flower," Annie smiled. "They make me think of somebody I used to know—a long time ago." She couldn't quite bring herself to mention her mother to this gay and giggly girl. Maybe, after they had known each other longer and become as good friends as Edith seemed to think they would be, she would tell Edith about the violet cologne her mother had used, and how just a faint whiff of that scent always brought back a crowd of happy memories. It was odd, she thought, that Edith had chosen this particular room for her. Maybe it was a good sign!

Tagg's room was right next to Annie's, through a connecting door. He stood in the doorway, and whistled admiringly. The wallpaper there was a mass of bright red roses, instead of violets. There were roses everywhere, on the walls, in the heavy gold-framed pictures, and embroidered on the silk lambrequin that was draped over the mantelpiece. "Wow!" he commented, and "Jingoes!"

Edith looked startled. Annie saw a little frown starting on her pretty face. "Tagg!" she reminded him, "where are your manners?" She turned to their hostess. "Tagg's trying to say how much he likes *his* room!"

Edith laughed and told Tagg gaily, "It's Papa's favorite, too. He loves roses!" Then she danced lightly toward the hall door. "Supper's at seven," she told them from the doorway. "You'll hear the bell. And do come right away, or Papa will be cross. He's such a fussbudget about everyone being on time!" She giggled again and fluttered away like a bright, harmless butterfly.

Annie closed the door and sternly pointed to the door to the rose room. "Scoot in there, punkins, and get washed. Those roses won't bite you. And don't make any smarty remarks about them to Edith."

"Okay, Sis," he grinned. "I won't say a word. But did

you notice all the furniture in there? Golly, there's enough for a whole house! Hope I don't walk in my sleep or I might break a leg."

"I'll break one for you, young feller!" Annie grabbed up a satin pillow that decorated the window seat. It had *Roses are red, Violets are blue* embroidered on it in gilt thread. She heaved it at Tagg, but he ducked out of sight. She heard him a minute later, pouring water into his washbowl, and making loud snortings and splashings which seemed to indicate that a thorough job of face-washing was going on.

But she knew her brother. She tiptoed to the doorway and peeked into the rose-y room. Sure enough, he was splashing the water in the bowl with his hands, and making bubbling noises, but his face and neck were still perfectly dry.

"What a busy little man!" she remarked. "Would you like big sister to help you, dear?"

Tagg jumped and went to work vigorously with the bar of yellow soap and the washcloth. He knew his ears would tingle for half an hour if she got to work on them. Annie grinned and withdrew.

Later, as she changed into her best starched white blouse

and a plain homespun skirt, she thought sadly about the long, unhappy day they had just gone through. She still wouldn't let herself have even one single doubt about Uncle Luke. She felt positive that Rango wasn't as honest as Mr. Shanley thought he was. If she could only figure how to find out more about him! She decided she would ask Mr. Shanley tonight at supper just how well he knew this man from Jumpoff.

She was still worrying, when the supper bell rang loudly at the foot of the stairs. She rounded up Tagg and hustled him down to join the Shanleys.

Edith and her father were waiting before the fireplace in the big reception hall. But Annie saw at once that she would have no chance to discuss Rango with Mr. Shanley, because Rango was a supper guest, too. She would have to wait till he left.

# 16          Annie Gets A Hunch

The Shanleys tried their best to make Annie and Tagg feel at ease at the supper table, but Rango's presence made it impossible. Edith was gay and playful, and chattered constantly, but even Tagg failed to laugh at her jokes. He was too busy scowling at Rango.

It was a relief to everyone when the meal was over. Edith led Annie and Tagg out onto the broad veranda to "catch the air" before bedtime, while the two men lighted their cigars and sauntered into the library.

Shanley could hardly wait to ask Rango what had happened this morning on the Jumpoff trail, Rango saw to it that the library door was tightly closed, before he gave Shanley the answer.

"The bullet that hit that outcrop of granite beside the trail was Rufe's first shot at MacTavish. He missed by six feet, and MacTavish had his six-gun out and was popping away across the canyon as quick as a flash. He yelled to me to hit the ground and roll behind a rock. That's what *he* tried to do." He paused to relight his cigar, and Shanley grunted impatiently.

"Go on! Then what?"

"I shot him myself." He said it matter-of-factly. "In the back."

Shanley winced. He knew Rango was cold-blooded. It had been useful to him. But there was something about shooting a man in the back—

Rango saw his reaction. He waved it off. "I had to. Both the Hortons were missing him a mile. Anyhow, he keeled over and rolled right off the edge of the trail. It's a long ways down, right there. You checked that."

Shanley nodded. "Yes, I know. Are you sure he was— uh—*finished?*"

Rango nodded vigorously. "I don't leave my jobs half done, Shanley," he boasted. "I climbed down as far as I could, about fifty feet. I could see the broken brush down below, where he fell through, but he'd dropped out of sight. It's about two hundred feet to the bottom there, at least, and he went all the way."

"But are you *sure?* And maybe your shot didn't hit him square."

"However it hit him, nobody's going to fall that far into a rocky-bottom arroyo, and live."

"I suppose not." Shanley still frowned.

"But *if* he still had some breath left when he hit bottom," Rango grinned, "it's a sure thing he's lost it by now. Because I left Rufe and Rube Horton out there to find him and see that he's laid under nice and proper."

"Well, in that case—" Shanley felt cheerful now. He gave Rango a handful of his best cigars. Everything was going to be all right now. It had been a profitable day.

Out on the wide veranda, Annie and Edith "visited" and rocked in the high-backed wicker chairs that had been one of the biggest sensations at the lawn party. They were the only two of their kind that the admiring Diabloites had ever seen west of the Missouri.

Tagg was feeling neglected, as Edith chatted on gaily about her school and her friends and her dresses. He listened from a lonely perch on the side railing, and wished he had eaten more supper. Rango being there had sort of spoiled his usual good appetite.

"Oh," Edith caught herself up suddenly with a pretty

gesture of confusion, "I'm so sorry! Here I've been rattling on about myself and I know you must be feeling just terrible about your uncle. Please forgive me!"

"It's all right." Annie smiled. "It was fun to hear about your school."

"I wish you could be going back with me this fall," Edith sighed. "But, of course, now, I suppose you wouldn't be able—Annie! Why don't you get rid of that silly little ranch—I know you could sell it for a good price, with all the new settlers coming out all the time. And you could leave Tagg here with Dad, and you could come back to school with me. We'd have a wonderful time!"

Annie shook her head. "My place is here in Diablo, with Tagg. I'll never sell the ranch."

Edith pouted prettily. "Please change your mind, Annie. We'd have such fun together!"

"As a matter of fact," Annie reminded her, "the ranch is Uncle Luke's property, not mine. I couldn't sell it to anyone if I wanted to."

"But if he's—I mean, if he doesn't come back, it'll be yours. You're his heirs, you and Tagg."

Annie nodded. "I suppose so, but I still feel that he's coming back. And when he does, I *know* he'll square himself."

Edith decided it was time to drop the subject. She would get to it another time.

"Oh, my dear! I do hope you're right, and the men are all wrong!" Then she waved her arm in a graceful gesture toward the moonlit garden, with its damply fragrant flowers and wide lawns. "Let's forget about it now, and just enjoy this moonlight! Isn't it heavenly?"

"Indians don't like moonlight!" Tagg jumped off his perch on the railing with a clatter. "They like it dark, so they can snee-eak up real quiet on the wagons, and scalp everybody and steal all the horses and cattle!"

"Oh!" Edith jumped to her feet and clapped her hands over her ears. "You horrid little boy! Talking about things like *scalping!* Ugh! I won't listen!" and she fled into the house in a flurry of rustling taffeta.

"Now you've done it, Mr. Tagg Oakley!" Annie kept the grin out of her voice. "You've got some apologizing to do."

"Aw, Annie," he was worried now, "I just thought maybe she'd like to know about Indians. I didn't mean to scare her away, honest." He gulped. "Shall I go tell her I'm sorry?"

"Never mind, hon. Tomorrow's time enough."

"Golly," he sat down, looking sad. "I hope she didn't mean what she called me. *Am* I a horrid little boy, Sis?"

"Of course not! She was just upset." Annie rumpled his hair, but he didn't grin back at her. Her heart went out to him. "Tell you what," she told him cheerfully, "we'll get the ponies saddled up and take ourselves for a fast little jaunt, just into town and back. And if the general store is still open, I'll squander a nickel on some peppermint lozenges. How's that?"

"Let's go!" He was halfway down the steps.

"Whoa there!" Annie picked up the kerosene lantern and the strip of sulphur matches that were always left handy to the porch. "I'll saddle up while you go up to my room and fetch my little change purse. I can't buy peppermints without money."

"Sure thing!" He made the steps two at a time.

"Wait!" Annie laughed at his eagerness. "Better bring my Springfield, too. No telling what we might run into."

He disappeared into the house and Annie took the lighted lantern with her to the barn. She was tired and worried but she wanted Tagg to go to bed happy. Their little gallop to Diablo and back should relax both of them.

She was still saddling the reluctant Pixie, who had

settled down to sleep and didn't want to be disturbed, when Tagg came down with the purse and the rifle. He sat down on the top step and hefted the heavy rifle. One of these days, Annie would let him shoot with it!

In the library, Dude Rango was getting ready to leave. "I still think you're making a mistake letting those Oakley kids stay here. Annie's got a sharp eye, and not much gets past her. She as good as called me a liar a couple of times, and the sooner you get her and the boy away from here, the safer you'll be."

But Shanley refused to worry. "Can't you see that by having those two here, I'm proving to everybody that I'm their friend in spite of what their crooked uncle has done to me? Why, Diablo will be buzzing about this tomorrow! And when I offer to take their miserable little ranch off their hands in a couple of weeks and send them back East to their relatives, that'll be final proof of my big generous heart! I'll be the town hero, no less!"

"I hope so!" Rango's tone indicated that he didn't agree. "You haven't much time left before those settlers start flocking out to claim their lots."

"I know! I know!" Shanley almost shouted. Rango irritated him sometimes.

"How about a couple of forged I.O.U.'s in the old man's writing? It would cut down the price you'll have to pay her for the ranch. And I'm handy with the pen, you know."

"Not necessary." Shanley waved it away.

Out on the veranda steps, Tagg was hunting a big grizzly bear while he waited for Annie to bring the horses for the ride to town. The clump of cactus beyond the well made a fine grizzly, if you didn't look too close. Tagg lifted the heavy Springfield to his shoulder and took wobbly aim.

"Bang!" He made believe he was pulling the trigger. "Gotcha that time, old bear!"

A hand came down over his shoulder and grabbed at the rifle. Tagg almost let go, in his surprise. Then he saw that it was Rango who was trying to take the gun, and he held on angrily, kicking at him and yelling, "Let go!"

"Let go yourself, pest! Or I'll—" Rango gave a final twist of the rifle and ripped it out of Tagg's hands. He started to examine it by the dim light of the veranda lamp. "Loaded, too. Don't you know it ain't safe for kids your size to have guns? I better keep this, so you won't hurt yourself."

"You give that back to me. It's my sister's!" Tagg was

trying to get his hands on the gun, and Rango was holding it away, high in the air.

"Or maybe I'll just fix it so you can't let it go off and do any damage." Rango pushed him aside so roughly that Tagg stumbled and almost fell. Then the wiry young gunman gripped the rifle by its barrel and started to smash it across the metal hitching post in front of the porch.

A rock hurtled out of the darkness from the direction of the barn. It caught Rango in the wrist and brought a yell of pain from his lips. He dropped the heavy Springfield, and grabbed his injured wrist.

Annie stepped quickly into the circle of light, grim-faced and angry. She retrieved her rifle while Rango was still nursing his wrist and glaring at her.

"Try bullying somebody your own size, mister," Annie told him. "Or maybe that's not your style!"

Rango glared, but the hasty arrival of John Shanley from inside the house stopped his angry reply before he had time to make it. "What's going on," Shanley demanded.

"Your friend Mr. Rango seemed to be trying to smash my rifle," Annie told him evenly. "But he gave it up."

"I wasn't going to smash it," Rango said angrily, "I was only joking with the boy."

"You joke sort of rough," Annie told him, and turned to
Tagg. "Did he hurt you?" Tagg shook his head, but he
stood close to her and stared defiantly at Rango. Annie took
his arm. "Reckon you'd better be turning in, punkin. We'll
let the ride go till tomorrow," she said. "It's been a long
day, and maybe we're all a mite edgy." She led him up the
steps. At the top she turned to look back at the two men.
"If you don't mind, Mr. Shanley, I'd like a word with
you—when Mr. Rango's gone." Then she disappeared into
the house with Tagg.

"I don't like the way she said that," Rango frowned.
"Sounds like she might have something figured out that we
don't know about."

Shanley nodded quickly. "It could be. Why don't you
wait around a while out by the barn? I'll run the shade up
in the library when she's done talking and gone to bed."

Rango agreed and rode away quickly, calling out his
good night so Annie would be sure to hear it. When he
got out beyond the big gates, he rode off into the night.
But a few minutes later he came back and dismounted in
the darkness beside the barn. He had a good view of John
Shanley's library window from that spot.

He lit a cigarette, and waited.

# 17 Trickery

"But I thought we were going to Diablo to buy some peppermints." Tagg had been holding back all the way up to his room. "You said we were. And I'm not tired, really." He had to stifle a yawn to say it.

Annie smiled and shook her head at him. "Well *I* am, young feller. The peppermints can wait till tomorrow. There's something I have to talk to Mr. Shanley about tonight, and it's getting late. So scoot along to bed and no more arguments."

"Pixie and Target are going to be disappointed," he made a last try, on the threshold of his room.

"I'll go right down and explain it to both of them," she grinned. "I think they'll be glad to get those saddles off again. Especially that lazy little Pixie of yours. I had an awful time getting his saddle onto him just now."

"Okay, Sis. I guess I am a mite sleepy."

She saw him tucked in bed and blew out the lamp at his bedside. "Don't get up till I call you in the morning," she told him as she kissed him good night. "There's no reason to be jumping around too early. I have a hunch the Shanleys sleep late, and we don't want to disturb them."

Tagg was sleepily saying his prayers as Annie tiptoed to her own room and softly closed the door that separated them.

She went down to the barn at once, to unsaddle the two horses and bed them down. Target wiggled his ears at her, and his big brown eyes seemed to be saying, "What kind of a game are we playing now? First you wake me up in the middle of the night and put that hot old saddle on me, and then you take it off again without giving me a chance to cool off on a nice moonlight ride!" Annie petted him and scratched his ears. "Human beings are all crazy, pony. Don't mind us."

As for Pixie, he had gone right back to sleep the moment the saddle was off. He was a calm little pony, and he took the strange actions of his human owners without question. Annie had decided long ago that he was a philosopher. Nothing bothered him, so long as he ate regularly.

As she closed the big barn doors and picked up her lantern to go back to the house, Annie stood still a moment,
and a puzzled frown came to her face. She was almost sure
that she could smell smoke, fresh cigarette smoke. She
looked around keenly, but there was no sign of anyone
near the barn. She even took a look along the shadowed side
of it, holding her lantern high. But no one was there, either.
She thought, "That's funny. The only person who smokes
cigarettes around here is that Mr. Rango, but he left quite
a while ago."

She listened hard a few seconds for the sound of a foot-
step, but all she heard was Target moving restlessly inside
the locked barn. So she started back to the house, swinging
her lantern and whistling faintly. But there was a slight
prickling down her spine as she went, and she had an
unpleasant feeling that someone was watching her every
step. Once she came to an abrupt stop and turned quickly,
lifting the lantern above her head, and scanning the quiet
yard through which she had just come. Nothing moved,
and no sound broke the stillness of the night except the
chorus of crickets in the damp shrubbery.

She left the lantern in its regular place and went on in to
Shanley's library. Her host was waiting. He was friendly

and cordial as ever, and invited her to be comfortable in one of the big leather chairs. There was even a glass of cool water, waiting for her beside the chair.

He smiled as she sipped the water. "And now, my dear child, what's troubling you so late in the night?"

She came to the point at once. "Mr. Shanley, I don't trust that Mr. Rango. I still don't believe that he's told us the truth about that ambush."

Shanley's smile faded as he listened. When she finished speaking, he was frowning. He rose from his chair and started to pace the room. Annie watched him and waited for his answer. When it came, it struck her that she had never noticed such a sharp tone in his voice before. He sounded angry with her.

"My dear girl," he scowled down at her, "I'm disappointed in you. I expected you to have more common sense. I know this thing about Luke has hit you hard, but you must face it squarely. We've been all over it once."

"I know how it looks," Annie was on the defensive, "but I still don't believe it."

"I have no reason to suspect Rango of lying. I told you what a big proposition he and I were planning, and I thought you realized how foolish any man would be to steal twenty thousand dollars when he had every prospect of making five or ten times that amount in a legitimate deal!" He frowned and made an impatient gesture. "I don't know what more I can say to convince you how unfair you're being to a man you know nothing about."

"That's just the point," Annie told him quietly. "I don't know anything about him, and I was wondering just how well *you* know him."

"Well," Shanley decided that he had better not go too fast till he found out what was in her mind, "I can't say I've known him long. We have mutual friends, of course, and they think a lot of him. I'm sure he's a solid citizen out at Jumpoff."

"He doesn't act like it, Mr. Shanley. I think he's fooling you."

"Why, that's ridicu—I mean, why do you think so, Annie?"

"I guess it's just a hunch—and what he did a little while ago to Tagg, trying to bust my rifle for no reason."

Shanley paced the floor in silence a moment. Then he faced Annie, frowning. "I'd like to believe that Luke didn't rob me, Annie. I'd far rather think this man, who's almost a stranger, did it. But the evidence is too strong."

"It may not be, after I've been to Jumpoff and asked a few questions about Mr. Rango and how he stands with the folks there!"

"Jumpoff!" Shanley didn't like this sudden turn. "You can't go to Jumpoff, asking questions about the man. You'll set people to talking there, and the first thing you know, you'll have spoiled Mr. Rango's chance to buy up those claims without starting a gold rush!" He shook his head vigorously. "No, Annie, I can't let you do any such thing."

"But don't you see—" she began.

"You're tired and hysterical, child. You've had a long hard day, and a lot of shocks. Now, be a good girl and go upstairs and try to get a good night's sleep. You'll see things clearer in the morning. And we'll have another talk. Maybe I'll even take a ride over to Jumpoff, myself in a couple of days, and make some inquiries. Just to put your mind at rest." He sighed and shook his head sadly. "Though I know it is a waste of time."

Annie got slowly to her feet and moved toward the door. Shanley watched her keenly. He hoped he had convinced her. He could pretend to take the long ride to Jumpoff some day next week, and show up again with glowing accounts of Rango's standing in the mining town.

But she turned at the door and looked back soberly. "I know you mean to do all you can to help Tagg and me, Mr. Shanley, and I sure thank you; but I've just got to go to Jumpoff myself and find out about Mr. Rango, one way or the other."

He smiled with an effort. "Well, I suppose it'll be all right for you to go with me. We'll take the buckboard, and Edith and Tagg can go along for the ride. We'd better make it Wednesday. I can close the office early."

Annie shook her head. "That's three days away. I'm sorry, Mr. Shanley, but I aim to go tomorrow morning." She saw his face darken, and added quickly, "I'll be very careful not to let out his secret about the gold strike. You can depend on it."

Shanley spoke harshly, with a scowl. "You're almost as stubborn as Luke MacTavish. I hope you'll think this over thoroughly tonight and change your mind. Jumpoff is a rough mining town, and no place for a young girl to go alone, if she values her good reputation!" He dismissed her with an abrupt wave of his hand. "Good night!"

Annie went slowly upstairs to her room. She *was* very tired and maybe a little hysterical, as Mr. Shanley had said. She would try to get some rest. A good sleep would help, but she was quite sure she wouldn't feel any different about riding to Jumpoff in the morning, no matter what anybody said. It was the only ray of hope she had left, and even if it made Mr. Shanley angry and impatient with her, she was going.

Downstairs, John Shanley listened to her door close before he went to the window and ran the shade up to the top to signal Dude Rango that it was safe to come back and hear what Annie had had on her mind.

It was long hours later when Rango slipped out of the side door and moved cautiously to his waiting horse. Dawn was showing in the east, but the shadows were still thick and dark under the trees. His well-trained horse stood patiently where Rango had left him, and the gun fighter made a quick mount. Then he did a strange thing.

He wheeled the startled animal, and digging his spurs into its flanks, rode at a gallop along the side of the house, past John Shanley's lighted library window. And as he rode by, he threw a rock through the glass, with a crash and tinkle that brought Annie out of bed, up in her second-floor room.

For a moment, she had no idea what had awakened her. Then she heard the pounding of hoofs on the graveled driveway, and John Shanley's voice shouting excitedly. She ran to the window and stared at the fast-moving figure of a mounted man, disappearing into the murky dawn shadows out at the big iron gates. He was too far away for her to make out what he or his horse looked like.

Downstairs, she could hear John Shanley reassuring the scared and sleepy servants that everything was all right and they were to go back to bed. She dressed quickly and started toward the door. Tagg, in his night clothes, was regarding her sleepily from the doorway between their rooms. "What was the racket?" he wanted to know.

"I'll let you know. Stay here till I come back."

In the upper hallway, she paused outside Edith's door. Not a sound in there! Edith had evidently slept through the commotion. It was just as well, if anything *was* wrong! Edith wouldn't be much help, and would most likely have a real case of hysterics.

Annie knocked at the library door, and John Shanley's voice called, "Come in!"

He was holding a small piece of rock in one hand, and staring with an expression of amazement and disbelief at the crumpled paper in his other hand. Behind him, the upper half of the window showed a smashed pane.

"Come in quickly, Annie. And close the door! This seems to be something—" his voice trailed off. He backed up to his desk chair and sat down heavily, staring at the paper in his hand. Annie hurried to him.

"What is it?" She guessed the meaning of the broken window pane. "Did somebody heave that rock through the window?"

Shanley nodded, and showed her the paper. "This was wrapped around it." .

"I saw someone riding out," she told him.

"Did you get a good look at him?" he demanded quickly.

She shook her head. "He was too far away, and it was too dark."

Shanley's heart stopped doing double time. "I didn't see the fellow, either. He rode by too fast. I was sitting here reading. I couldn't sleep, after all that happened yesterday. I thought I'd read till my nerves settled down. Then, just as I was about to put out the lamp on my desk here, a few minutes ago, I heard somebody ride by and this rock crashed through the window."

"What does the paper say?"

"It's—" John Shanley looked down again at the paper

and frowned. When he looked up into Annie's worried eyes, his face was grim. "It's—it's a confession, Annie. The man who robbed me wrote it."

She sensed by his expression what was coming.

"It's signed by Luke MacTavish."

"Uncle Luke!"

John Shanley nodded. His voice was harsh. "This leaves us no doubt. He's put it all in black and white."

There was still one chance. "How do you know he wrote it? Let me see! I know Uncle Luke's writing. They can't fool me on it! Tagg and I have had too many letters from him!"

Shanley handed the letter to her without a word. This was the moment, he thought. Was Rango as good a forger as he boasted he was?

He watched her closely as she studied the crumpled page.

"I—I guess he wrote this, all right," her voice sounded small and lost. "It's his writing. But—I can't believe what he says."

"It's hard, I know." Shanley's voice held just the right tinge of regret. "But, there it is!"

Annie read it silently. The words stood out in Luke's rounded, almost childish script, black and convincing. *John,*

she saw there, *I am sending this by one of my men, to put you straight. I got your twenty thousand. You were a fool to let me talk you into sending me along to guard it. You should have listened to Ben Crane after I got away with his payroll. Too bad, but I need your cash to pay off my gang. When you get this I'll be safe over the border to stay. One more thing. I got a deal for you. One time you said you'd buy my Bull's-Eye spread. It ain't worth much, but you might get a few thousand out of it if you cut it up into lots. It's yours free and clear if you promise me to ship the Oakley kids back where they came from. Tell Annie I said for her and Tagg to sign a quit claim. And get them on their way east as soon as you can. Luke MacTavish.*

Shanley sat quietly while Annie read the letter over twice. He could see how shocked she was at its revelations. He silently congratulated himself and the skillful Rango for their successful job on it. It hadn't been easy to get just the right words into that letter, words that would convince her of her uncle's guilt, and at the same time goad her into agreeing to sign a deed to the ranch and get out of Diablo as soon as possible. But it was working!

She sat white-faced and stunned as she finished reading. He leaned over to her and patted her hand. "Poor child," he said. "I wish you could have been spared this!"

Annie tried to hold her head up, but it was just too much for her. Suddenly her face was buried on her arms on Shanley's desk, and great sobs were shaking her slim young body.

He watched her, a cynical smile twisting his lips. Now, he reflected, there would be an end to her talk about riding to Diablo to check on Rango's standing there.

He reached into his humidor for a cigar. Then he drew back his hand. It might not look right to be puffing a cigar just now. He closed the silver-mounted humidor and pushed it away from him. "Poor child!" he repeated, in a voice vibrant with sympathy. "My heart aches for you and the little fellow!"

# *18*                      Fate Takes a Hand

It was for only a few short moments that Annie let the shock of her uncle's "confession" get the better of her. Then she dried her eyes and courageously faced up to the situation.

"What Uncle Luke said—there—about your taking over the ranch—" she began. It was still hard for her to talk about it.

"Go on, my dear," John Shanley spoke sympathetically.

"I mean, the ranch isn't worth nearly as much as he—stole," she got the word out with difficulty, "is it?"

"No, not by quite a few thousand dollars. Though, as he suggests, I might subdivide the quarter section that's on the edge of town, and make a little by selling the lots. But if you and Tagg want to stay on, of course you needn't sign over the ranch."

Annie shook her head. "No, thanks, Mr. Shanley. We

won't want to stay around here any longer than we have to, now."

"Suit yourself, my dear girl," he was careful to keep a sad note in his voice. "I can see how you children would feel. Diablo folks might not be very friendly." He added hastily, "Not that they would blame you two."

"I know." Annie thought about Ben Crane and the other men in the posse who had been so ready to believe her uncle was a crook. "It's only natural."

She started slowly toward the door and then stopped. "Just what do Tagg and I do about deeding you the ranch?"

"Well, let's see now," he studied over it, as if he hadn't already planned it out. "Perhaps I'd better have my lawyer draw up a legal paper on it—some day soon."

"Today would be best." Annie saw no reason to put it off, now everything was settled.

"All right, my child, if you say so. I can probably find time for it today."

"Thank you." Annie tried to smile back at him from the open door.

"Now, do try to get some sleep the rest of the night. And after breakfast, we'll talk about the arrangements."

Tagg was waiting impatiently in her room. "Golly, I

thought you'd never get back up here!" he complained. "What was all the excitement?"

"Nothing much," she tried to make it sound gay, "just a man with a letter for Mr. Shanley."

"So late at night? Jiminy, it must have been important! What was in it?"

"I told you it was for Mr. Shanley, button. Do I read other people's mail?" She laughed, but it sounded flat even to herself. "Now, scoot back to bed, and let me get a couple of hours' sleep."

But Tagg knew something was wrong. "You'd better tell me, Annie. It's something bad, isn't it? Your eyes are red around the edges, like you've been crying."

"Me?" she tried again to laugh, but Tagg shook his head slowly at her, and his freckled little face was dead serious.

"You told me not to fib, this afternoon, 'cause the truth always fits better. Now you're trying to fib, yourself. You shouldn't, Annie."

She sat down beside him, on the fancy satin pillow, and put her arm around him. "I'm not going to, honey. It's pretty bad news, but you'll hear it soon anyhow, so I might as well give it to you straight out." And she told him about the rider who had brought the confession, and about her talk with John Shanley, and what they had decided. When she had finished, Tagg sat staring at the big bunches of purple violets on the wallpaper, and for a moment he didn't say anything.

Then he spoke in a tired little voice, "How soon can we go away from here?"

"Pretty quick, hon," she answered. "There are some papers to sign, like Uncle's letter said we should. And we'll go out to the ranch and pack up our things. And then in a few days, maybe, we'll be driving that old mule wagon again, and riding along on our ponies." She spoke cheerfully.

He turned and studied her face. "But where will we be heading, Annie?"

She looked into his troubled eyes, and her own were bright with courage. "Now, what's it matter *where?* We'll be together, same as we've always been. And we'll be okay!"

It was late in the morning before Annie and Tagg came sleepily down to the big cool dining room. The sullen servant girl told them that John Shanley had breakfasted early and gone to his office at Diablo. As for Miss Edith, the girl had no idea when she would be up and around. Or if she had, she was not bothering to answer any questions about it. She slammed their breakfast down in front of them and swept starchily back into the kitchen, closing the door firmly after her.

"She acts like she's heard the news about Uncle Luke," Tagg remarked, poking disgustedly at a cold fried egg.

Annie nodded. "Never mind, punkins," she told him. "We'll soon be away from Diablo for good."

Tagg took a small drink of milk. Even that tasted as if it had been around a long time. He shoved himself back from the table. "Let's get out to the ranch." He looked around the big room with its gleaming silver on the big sideboard and its heavy velvet curtains. "I don't think I like it here any more."

Annie couldn't help agreeing with him on that. There was still no sound from Edith's room as they repacked the heavy old carpetbag that was all they had brought from the ranch. They were soon saddling up at the barn.

As she led Target outside, Annie stopped a moment to study something on the ground beside the barn door. There were four partly smoked cigarettes lying close together and several burned-out sulphur matches nearby. Someone had waited here. Quite a while, too. And his horse had been tied close by.

It must have been the man who brought the letter, she decided. She stooped and picked up one of the stubs, gingerly. It wasn't the kind the cowboys roll for themselves, out of brown paper and loose tobacco. It was the machine-made kind, with a name printed on it. Somewhere lately, she had noticed somebody smoking that kind of cigarette. She couldn't quite bring to mind who it was. It would probably come back to her later. Meanwhile, she and Tagg had to get over to the ranch and start packing.

They rode down the winding carriage driveway toward the tall iron gates. Tagg glanced back at the big house with its cupola and ornate veranda. He startled Annie by waving to someone there. She turned to look, and was in time to see the lace curtains on one of Edith's windows drop into place. Tagg was grinning.

"I guess Edith isn't mad at me any more," he said cheerfully. "She was smiling at us."

Annie nodded. "That's good," she told him. But she wondered to herself what kind of a smile it had been. She was beginning to think that Edith had deliberately avoided them this morning.

It was only a short ride to the ranch house. Things looked just the same as they had yesterday. The cow was mooing unhappily in her stall, and Annie got to work at once with the milking, while Tagg took care of the patient mules.

They were still busy around the barn when Annie heard the clop-clop of hoofs and the heavy rumble of a big wagon coming into the ranch yard. She glanced out and saw an old-time "burden wagon" with its canvas top and its high side ribs. A span of oxen were pulling it, and a thin-faced elderly woman in a red and green sunbonnet was driving.

Annie hurried out of the barn to give the stranger a greeting. It was not unusual for immigrants to stop by a ranch and rest their animals and themselves for a few hours of "visitin' " before they went on westward. Annie was glad there was plenty of cool water in the well, and a generous supply of food.

The gaunt settler woman climbed down from her high perch with a series of groans and grunts, and stood rubbing her tired arms. "Them oxen," she said, with a tinge of bitterness, "is the stubbornest critters alive . . . barrin' menfolks." She threw a disgusted look toward the canvas wagon-top. "They near pulled m'arms outa joint. They was dead set on goin' past here, an' I was jist as set on stoppin' and askin' the way."

There was a stir inside the wagon, and a moment later a red-bearded face appeared between the canvas curtains behind the high seat.

"What for are we stoppin', Amanda?" The faded blue eyes above the red beard were childishly reproachful. "You said we'd be gittin' to the town 'fore nighttime so I could buy me some medicine."

"That we will, David Jonathan Sam'l Brewster. Jist you rest quiet a while longer, and save your stren'th." The head disappeared and the curtains closed. The woman turned to Annie with a sigh. She indicated the curtains with a wave of her hand. "Husband," she announced. "Got the rheumatics right bad. Misery all the time. Can't handle the reins any more."

Annie made a sympathetic sound. "This country's good for rheumatics and such," she said. "He'll be feeling better in a few shakes of a lamb's tail."

"Hope so," said Mrs. David Jonathan Samuel Brewster, but she didn't look as if she thought there was much chance of it. She seemed tired and discouraged, and her big bony hands were calloused and worn.

"Got far to go?" Annie asked.

"Town called Diablo. They told us back at Smoke Tree

Station it was on this road, about fifteen miles."

"Oh, you're practically there," Annie said cheerfully. "You can make it in just a little while. But you better have something cool first."

"Don't mind if I do." The gaunt woman swung along at Annie's side as they headed for the porch. "We come all the way from the east coast. Far as Kansas City by railroad coach. Bought this wagon there." She glanced back at it with pride. "All our stuff's in it. My black haircloth sofy, that Ma gave me for a weddin' present. An' our steel engravin' of George Washin'ton crossin' the Delaware. An' my luster teapot, an' David Jonathan's fiddle."

"How did you pick Diablo to come to?"

"Saw the advertisement in our town paper. Writ out to ask about it, an' next thing we knew, we had ourselves a nice piece of land, like we've been dreamin' about for years."

"Oh, you bought it by mail?" Annie was enjoying the friendly visit. It helped her put her own troubles out of her mind.

"Sure did, honey," the woman chuckled. She reached into the oversized knitting bag she had been clutching grimly ever since she had climbed down off the wagon.

She brought out a well-worn big manila envelope, and burrowed in it. "I'll show you where it is on the map."

Annie went to get a cool glass of water and a plate of cookies. Mrs. Brewster was still searching for her map when Annie came back and set them on the porch table. The visitor had donned a battered old pair of glasses with a warped metal frame, and was peering over them at the jumbled contents of the envelope. Suddenly she gave a grunt of triumph and dug out a thin sheet of parchment paper that showed signs of much handling. Its edges were frayed and its creases so deep that it was almost ready to fall apart. But the map was neatly drawn and lettered and the words *City of Diablo* stood out clear and bold.

Annie studied it while her guest nibbled on a raisin cooky. "This is Diablo, all right. Here's the general store. . . ."

Mrs. Brewster pointed a long skinny finger at the map. "We figger after a while to open a barbershop along about here in town. Mr. Shanley says he has places to rent."

"Mr. Shanley?" Annie was pleased to hear they had bought their land from her friend Shanley. "We know him well."

"He's the one sold us our lot," the older woman nodded.

"From what he wrote us, I guess most everybody in the Territory thinks pretty highly of him." She looked suddenly worried. "I hope he won't be too riled up at us for doin' what he told us not to."

"What was that?" Annie was surprised.

"Comin' out here before the weather turned cool. He wrote us not to get started till along in late fall, when the heat was gone. Said the desert was so hot this time o' year nobody ever tried to cross it."

"It *was* hot, wasn't it?" Annie thought it was nice of Shanley to warn them.

"We got through without too much trouble," Mrs. Brewster answered. "Wasn't as bad as he said. Anyhow, we couldn't wait. David Jonathan's rheumatics was actin' up pretty bad and the doctor bills was gettin' out of hand. So I got to thinkin' that the sooner I fetched him out here to the desert air, hot or not, the better. I made up my mind to start right off no matter what Mr. Shanley said."

"And you made it!" Annie could picture what that journey had been, with the sickly, nearly helpless man.

"It took pretty near all our money to git here," Mrs. Brewster confided. "Lucky we're close to the end of our trip." Her finger stabbed the map, close to the edge. An

area was circled neatly with red ink and marked in neat
lettering, *D. Brewster lot, 100 by 200. Paid.* "There we are,
just outside of the east end of town. About a quarter mile,
Mr. Shanley said in his letter."

"That's in this direction," Annie said. "Let's see. . . ."
She stopped abruptly and frowned at the map. "Why!
according to this—" She jumped to her feet and stepped
to the edge of the porch. "Tagg!" she called. "Come here
a minute!"

Tagg came reluctantly. He had been sitting in the shade
of the big wagon, listening to Mr. Brewster relate some
hair-raising experiences he had endured on the long trip.
Tagg knew he was making up most of them, but he had
been waiting till Mr. Brewster stopped to catch his breath,
and he could get a word of his own in about his and Annie's
own recent journey. But Annie's call came while the visitor
was still talking.

Annie handed him the map. "Take a look at this, button.
There's the piece of land these folks have bought from
Mr. Shanley for their home. Where do you figure it is?"

He studied it, proud that she had called him for an
opinion. "Let's see, now. There's Little Dry Wash, running across it. . . ." He paused to grin at Mrs. Brewster.

"You don't have much farther to go." Then he took another look at the map and turned a puzzled face to Annie. "That's funny, Sis," he said. "I thought Little Dry Wash was *inside* Uncle Luke's boundary line."

Annie took the map from his hand. "It is," she answered. "Little Dry Wash is part of this ranch." She turned abruptly to the surprised woman. "Mr. Shanley has sold you folks a piece of land that he didn't own!"

# 19          A Tangled Web

The gaunt settler woman stared at Annie in dismay. She took the map and studied it closely, while Annie traced the Bull's-Eye boundary for her. The piece of ground into which she and her invalid husband had put all their savings was well inside the ranch's western border.

"But this feller Shanley wrote he owned all the land east of Diablo City for a couple miles. You sure he didn't buy this place from your uncle, miss?"

"No." Annie was beginning to put the pieces of the puzzle together in her mind and it was making a picture of John Shanley that she could hardly believe. "He tried to buy it months ago, but my uncle wouldn't sell."

"So the buzzard went ahead an' took our money, for something he had no rights to! Where can I see that land shark?" She was on her feet ready to go and do battle right now. "I'll give him a lesson he ain't goin' to forgit, about rookin' poor sick folks!"

"Please—wait a minute, Mrs. Brewster." Annie was still reluctant to face it. "Maybe at the time Mr. Shanley advertised he thought Uncle was going to sell him the land any day."

"That don't excuse him," Mrs. Brewster's tired face was stony. "He cheated us. And I bet we ain't the only ones! No wonder he wanted us to wait till fall. Give him more time to try to get hold of your ranch before we could git here to claim our land!"

"My brother and I are giving the ranch to him today— to make up for something my Uncle Luke did."

"That don't change things for us!" Mrs. Brewster's voice broke. "The deed we got for our money is no good, because the land wasn't his when he made the deal."

"He'll give you a new deed, as soon as Tagg and I sign over the ranch," Annie assured her. "I'll get his promise on that before I put my name on any papers."

"That's right obligin' of you, miss," she was pathetically grateful. "It was lucky we stopped by here."

"How do we know he won't hold us up on the price?" asked the husband. "We can't pay any more."

"I don't think he will," Annie answered with quiet assurance. "He won't want any talk to get around."

She glanced at the sky. By the height of the sun, it was getting along toward noon. Mr. Shanley should be back at his house by now, with the quit claim papers for Tagg and her to sign. She wanted to get this settled.

"You folks just make yourselves at home here," she told the Brewsters. "We'll be back in a little while. And don't worry, Mrs. Brewster, we'll see it's all ironed out for you."

Mr. Brewster was stretched out comfortably on the porch in Uncle Luke's favorite chair, and Mrs. Brewster was pumping up a fresh bucket of well water, as Annie and Tagg started their ponies on the way back to the Shanley home.

"That was a funny kind of thing for Mr. Shanley to do," Tagg commented, "selling what didn't belong to him. That's a crime, isn't it, Annie?"

She nodded. "Reckon it is. But maybe he didn't mean it to be. We mustn't ever judge folks till we hear all sides of a story."

There was no sign of John Shanley's return from town, as the Oakleys rode up to the shady veranda of the big house. The short ride under the summer desert sun had left Pixie and Target hot and thirsty.

"Better take them to the barn for a drink," Annie told her brother, "after they've cooled down a bit. I'll go on in and see if Edith's around. Maybe she'll know when her father will be back from town."

There was no reply to her light tap on Edith's door, but she was sure that she could hear someone stirring around in there. If Edith wanted to be childish and refuse to speak to her, there was nothing Annie could do but go away again. She felt a pang as she thought how happy she had been at the prospect of friendship with a girl her own age in Diablo. "Oh, well," she told herself, "I suppose she's upset over Uncle Luke."

The library looked cool and dark, and she decided to wait in there for Mr. Shanley to arrive. She sat down in his big leather desk chair and leaned far back, the way she had seen him do. It was nice and comfortable.

She thought a little drowsily that some day she would like to get Uncle Luke a chair like this instead of that hard wooden-backed rocker of his!

But the thought vanished as the recollection jolted her, suddenly, that Uncle Luke wouldn't be needing it. He was somewhere down over the border, running from the law.

And if they found him, he would be in prison for a long time.

She felt her eyes filling with tears, and told herself fiercely, "Stop feeling sorry for yourself, Annie Oakley. You came here to finish up some business, not to cry!" And she hurriedly sat up straight, and swung the oversized chair around on its swivel, so she could step out of it. But she pushed it a little too hard, and she kept on going the whole way around. By the time she had clutched the edge of the desk and stopped herself, her foot had knocked over a metal wastepaper basket beside the desk. She got out of the chair and knelt to replace the scrap paper she had spilled out of the basket. "Clumsy!" she scolded herself. And she hoped Mr. Shanley wouldn't come in and catch her scrabbling around on his floor. It would be too humiliating to explain.

She rammed the crumpled papers back into the wastebasket, a handful at a time. All at once she stopped and stared at the sheet she held in her hand. Something about it looked familiar. She smoothed it out and stared at it in stunned surprise.

*Dear John, I am sending*— the line at the top of the page read. It looked like Uncle Luke's writing, a little. There was a second line under the first. *Dear John, I am sending this letter—* The word "letter" was crossed out. A third line read, *Dear John, I am sending this by one of my men—* This time, the writing looked even more like Uncle Luke's.

"Those are the words Uncle Luke wrote in that letter he sent last night," she thought, staring at them. "And it looks like his writing—" Suddenly it all came clear to her. Uncle Luke hadn't sent John Shanley a confession at all! It had been written right here by somebody else who copied Uncle Luke's writing and signed it with his name! This crumpled paper was the sheet that the one who wrote that letter used, to practice his forgery on!

Then the man who rode by and threw the rock and the letter through the window was a fake! He wasn't a messenger from Uncle Luke at all! And if *he* was a fake, and the confession was a forgery, done right here in Mr. Shanley's library, that meant Shanley was in on it, all the way! And instead of being Uncle Luke's friend and hers and Tagg's, he was a liar and a cheat!

A sudden realization made her gasp. If the confession was a lie, as this crumpled paper proved beyond a doubt, then the whole story Shanley had told her about Uncle Luke must be a web of lies! And instead of having ambushed

Rango out on the trail, Uncle Luke may have been the one who was waylaid!

It was terribly clear. Poor Uncle Luke had been tricked into offering to guard Mr. Shanley's money, and then he had been robbed of it. And the confession had been faked so that she would believe it and hand over the property to Mr. Shanley without checking on Rango. She knew now from the Brewsters why John Shanley needed Uncle Luke's ranch. And there were probably half a dozen other buyers just like those poor folks.

But where was Uncle Luke now? What had they done to him out there on the Jumpoff trail yesterday?

As she started for the door, with the paper in her hand, she heard the clicking of high heels along the hallway. Then the door was flung open, and Edith stood there glaring accusingly at her. "I thought so!" she sneered. "I knew when I saw you two sneaking back here, that you were up to something!"

"We didn't sneak back, Edith," Annie tried to hold her voice level. "I came to see your father about the ranch."

"And you thought you'd do some snooping while you were here!" Edith sneered. She pointed scornfully to the papers strewn around the floor beside the wastebasket.

"I wasn't snooping, but I sure found something!" Annie's anger flared.

"You better be careful, or you'll end up in prison, the way your precious uncle is going to!"

"If anybody goes to prison around here, it won't be me or my Uncle Luke!" She flashed the paper at Edith.

Edith's mouth twisted scornfully. Annie wondered how she had ever thought Edith was pretty. "I don't know what you're trying to invent," Edith said curtly, "but it won't do you any good. Everybody in Diablo County knows your uncle is a criminal, and in my opinion you and that horrid little ragamuffin Tagg are no better!" Her eyes blazed. "You're a pair of common little upstarts, and I wouldn't put anything past you!"

"At least, we'd draw the line at forgery, Miss Shanley!" Annie spoke bluntly. She waved the wrinkled paper in Edith's face. "That's what your father has been up to. And this is the proof of it!"

"Nothing but lies, of course!" Edith shrugged it off, disdainfully.

"I don't have to lie," Annie answered quietly. "It's here in black and white." And she started to fold the paper to put it into the pocket of her riding skirt.

The moment Annie took her eyes off Edith, the girl's hand darted out and snatched the paper away from her. Then Edith whirled and ran swiftly out the door.

Annie ran after her along the hall and up the stairs. She was close behind as Edith darted into her own room and slammed the door. Annie threw herself against it before Edith could turn the key in the lock.

As she pushed the door wide, she saw Edith dash across the room to the fireplace, where a tiny flame was still flickering from her breakfast fire. Before Annie could get to her, Edith had flung the sheet of paper onto the flame.

"There!" she laughed triumphantly into Annie's angry face.

Annie grabbed her arm and pulled her away roughly from in front of the fire. Edith stumbled as one of her high heels caught in the deep pile of the carpet, and she fell with an angry shriek, face down across her cushion-piled day bed. Annie knelt at the fireplace and hurriedly tried to rake out the burning paper, but it had too good a start, and it went up in smoke before she could rescue it. She jumped to her feet as she heard the door behind her slam. Edith was gone, and the key was turning in the lock outside. She heard Edith's heels click away down the hall.

She hurried to the window and flung it open. There wasn't even a small porch outside of Edith's room, or vines she could use to climb down on. She looked quickly for Tagg but he was evidently still in the barn. She hoped he would show up soon, so he could help her get out of there. Shanley might be arriving any minute, and she had a feeling that she had better not be locked in here after he came home and heard Edith's story. She felt for her gun belt, and remembered with a sinking feeling that she had left it, with her six-shooter, hanging on the pommel of Target's saddle when she sent Tagg out to the barn with the two horses.

If Shanley had turned on his former friend, Luke Mac-Tavish, had waylaid and made him a prisoner, or even had him killed, there was no telling how he would treat her and Tagg when they refused to sign over the ranch to him. And they *would* refuse—no matter what he did.

There was still no sign of Tagg over at the barn. She could only wait, and wonder how much time they still had to get away before Shanley came.

But John Shanley was in no hurry to go home today. He was in a celebrating mood. He had just been down the street to his lawyer's office to get the quit claim paper drawn up for the Oakley pair to sign. And on the way there and back to his office, he had made several stops to show the dramatic confession that "one of Luke MacTavish's gang" had thrown through his window last night. The whole town was buzzing with the news.

Rango's feet were on one end of the desk, and Shanley had so far forgotten his usual pompous dignity as to swing his feet up on the other.

"Well, that's another good job done," Rango yawned. "How about my small wages, boss?"

Shanley laughed and swung his feet down. He turned to the heavy iron safe and started to swing the shiny knob right and left. "You earned them this time, my boy. Don't squander it all at once." He took out a sheaf of crisp paper money and laid it on his desk.

Rango grinned. "I'll buy me one of those 'gold claims' at Jumpoff that we baited the hook with to land Mac-Tavish!"

He laughed at his own joke as he held out his hand for the money. Shanley joined in the gunslinger's laughter, and started counting out the thousand dollars he had promised him.

Both men went suddenly silent at the sound of a soft

tapping on the alley door. It came again, three light raps and then two more.

"Must be Rufe or Rube," Rango whispered.

Shanley stuffed the currency into his pocket and kicked the big safe door shut. Then he went to the door and opened it. One of the Horton twins, dirty and grimy, his clothes gray with dust, stood there.

"What are you doing in town? Why didn't you wait till after dark to come here?"

Horton stepped inside, wiping the sweat off his forehead with a dirty shirt sleeve. "Bad news." His voice was hoarse.

"Where'd you find MacTavish?" Rango came to the point at once. "Did you put him under okay?"

Rube Horton shook his head. Both men stiffened.

"What do you mean by that?" Shanley barked.

"Well," Rube wasn't enjoying his errand, "he was hit, right enough. Rango's shot tumbled him over the edge, and he fell straight down. Looked like he'd be finished, anyhow, when we found him, so me an' Rufe, we kinda took our time gettin' down to him. It was brutal hot yesterday, an' mean weather to go climbin' around them hot rocks."

"Go on!" Shanley mashed his expensive cigar into a

shapeless mass in the ash tray. "Come to the point."

"Why, when we got down there, where he landed, he wa'n't there! There was plenty of signs, though. We could see he'd been hit bad, an' we figgered he couldn't have dragged off too far. So we set out lookin' fer him, Rufe up one way an' me the other. But we lost him in them rocks an' gullies." He shook his head sadly. "An' then it come on to turn dark, so we give up for the night, an' made camp."

Shanley's face was black with anger and growing fear. "What about this morning? Did you locate him?"

Rube looked unhappy. "Nope! Didn't see hide nor hair of him. Seems like he jist disappeared into thin air."

"That means he's still alive down there!" Shanley turned on Rango. "I left it up to you to do the job, and you let these half-wits bungle it. Do you know what will happen if MacTavish shows up again, alive and talking?"

Rango nodded uneasily. "Yeah—but we know he's hit bad. There's no chance he can make it up out of there."

"There's always a chance! But we'll take care of that right now. We're going to comb the bottom of that canyon till we find him." He smiled, an unpleasant smile. "You'll be paid when the job is finished—and not before." He threw the money back into his safe and slammed the door.

A little later, John Shanley and Rango rode past the jail together. Lofty Craig was lounging unhappily on the steps. He looked as if he had lost his last friend. He glanced up at John Shanley and called, "How are Annie and Tagg takin' the news?"

Shanley answered him, sadly, "I'm going out to see them at my house, right now. They were feeling pretty bad about it when I left this morning."

As he rode on, he told Rango, "We'll stop by the house and get them to sign this quit claim on the ranch. I want that settled now."

Rango nodded. "Sure. There's no rush getting out to Jumpoff. Rube's on his way, and maybe by the time he gets there, Rufe'll have MacTavish spotted."

"Let's hope so," Shanley answered, sourly.

## 20                         The Hill Trail Again

Pixie and Target had enjoyed their rest in the cool Shanley barn. Tagg led them over toward the house at a leisurely stroll. He hoped that Annie had finished talking about the Brewsters to Mr. Shanley. He didn't feel very happy, hanging around here now.

Annie's shrill whistle made him look around quickly. For a moment, he couldn't see her. Then he did. She was leaning out of one of Edith's windows and waving him over hastily. He ran to see what was wrong. The two ponies trotted after him.

Annie leaned far out. "Bring Target close under this window!"

Tagg stared up. "What for?"

"Don't argue! Just do it!" She was already starting to climb out onto the window sill, a knotted length of Edith's

elegant bed sheet in her hand. Inside the room, she had tied
one end to the high post of Edith's heavy carved bedstead.

Annie swung down on the sheet as Tagg brought Target
up. The sheet rope was several feet short, but she dropped
off the end and landed in her saddle. "Hurry!" she called
to Tagg, as she buckled on her gun belt. "We've got to get
out of here fast!"

Tagg made a quick mount, and together they cut across
the expensive Shanley lawn and onto the gravel driveway.
They were cantering out through the tall iron gates as
Edith ran onto the porch and stood glaring after them.

"Oh!" she exclaimed, and "Oh!" with an angry stamp
of her delicate little foot. But there was nothing she could
do to stop them.

As they rode, Annie told Tagg about the evidence of
forgery she had found in Shanley's library basket, and how
Edith had burned it. He was happy to know that his uncle
wasn't a robber, and he was fiercely angry with the
treacherous Shanley. But Annie could see that it was Edith's
actions that upset him the most. "Golly!" he mourned.
"I never thought *she* would do anything mean like that
to us!"

Annie couldn't help smiling to herself in spite of the

gravity of the situation. "Just like a man," she thought, "even if he's only fryin' size! A pretty face'll fool 'em every time!"

They were at the turn of the road where the trail to Jumpoff cut off into the hills. Annie pulled up quickly and laid her hand on Pixie's bridle. "Wait," she told Tagg. "I just remembered something. The one I saw smoking those machine-made cigarettes yesterday was Rango! So he could be the feller that waited out by Shanley's barn last night! It adds up!"

"Sure!" Tagg agreed eagerly. "And he tried to break your rifle so you couldn't use it! But you can handle *him* if he tries to keep us from finding Uncle Luke!"

"We can't be sure he'd give me the chance," she answered gravely. "I think you'd better circle back to town and find Lofty. Tell him what's up and tell him to round up a posse and come on out to the Jumpoff trail again. Steer clear of the Shanley place, and get to the jail by way of the alley, in case Mr. Shanley's still in his office."

"Why can't I go with you? I can help, honest!"

"You'll help more by seeing that posse gets started, pronto. Now scoot! A good soldier never questions his orders—remember that!"

Tagg saluted the way Colonel Oakley had taught him, long ago, and Annie solemnly returned his salute. Then Tagg wheeled Pixie and headed back to Diablo at a gallop.

Annie gave a little sigh of relief as she glanced back and watched him disappearing. Now, if she ran into trouble, she wouldn't worry about the little feller. As she rode, she checked over her rifle and the six-shooter in her holster. There was no telling what she might find waiting for her out there.

It was only a few minutes after the Oakleys had left, that John Shanley rode up to his house with Dude Rango.

Edith ran out to meet them, and told her father about Annie finding the paper in his wastebasket. Shanley's face darkened with anger as he turned on Rango. "I thought you destroyed those old papers!" he snarled.

"And I thought you were going to do it after I left!" Rango scowled right back at him.

"I suppose she rushed right to town with it," Shanley was really worried. "Strange we didn't meet her."

Edith laughed shrilly and tossed her curls. Her father glared at her. "Are you out of your mind? Don't you realize how serious this is?"

Edith stared coldly back at him. "I didn't get a chance to

finish telling you what happened," she said. "She doesn't have the paper any more. I snatched it from her and burned it!"

"Burned it!"

She nodded with a smug expression. "I can show you the ashes in my fireplace!"

"Then we're in the clear!" Rango was grinning now. "Nobody'll believe her without that paper. They'll think she made up the whole story."

"And I'll see that they do!" Shanley chuckled. "It'll be my word against hers, and I hardly think anyone will take her seriously under the circumstances."

Rango shrugged. "You still don't have her name on that quit claim," he reminded Shanley.

"I don't believe she'll give us any trouble when it comes to a showdown. I'll make her and the boy a present of a few hundred dollars, out of the bigness of my heart, when I see them on their way back East!"

"You have all the answers, Shanley," Rango laughed, "but how about finishing that little hunting trip we were talking about, before you start counting your profits?"

Their eyes met over Edith's curly head. Shanley nodded grim agreement.

A few minutes later they were on their way up toward the high trail to Jumpoff. "We'll get this settled first," Shanley said as they rode through the hills behind Diablo. "Then there'll be no more surprises turning up!"

A long way ahead of them on the narrow, dusty trail, Annie had reached the scene of the ambush. No sound broke the stillness as she brought the pony to a stop opposite the granite outcrop on the far canyon wall. This was the place they had visited yesterday with Rango.

She slid out of the saddle and looked for a place to hide Target. A rock-filled gully a few feet wide came down steeply from the brush-grown crown of the hill. Thirty or so feet up there, Target would be out of sight of anyone who came up the trail.

She took the pony carefully up the wash and tied him in the shade of a small live-oak sapling. It was the only cool spot around. She gave him a lump of sugar, a friendly pat, and a whispered warning not to whinny when he got lonesome. Then she made a quick descent, rifle in hand. When she glanced up from the bottom of the trail, she was happy to see he was entirely hidden.

She started to search for some clue as to what had really happened around there to Uncle Luke. But it was no use.

The posse had trampled the ground and stamped out any signs that might have been of help.

Then she noticed something she had overlooked before. The brush at the edge of the trail was broken. Something heavy had lain on it. And the ground underneath was stained a dark brown. She felt sick. She was pretty sure she knew what that stain meant.

She saw the imprints of booted feet on the edge a little farther along. They seemed to lead down over the edge. She parted the low bushes and peered down. Directly below her, there was a narrow ledge, and it wound down like a footpath against the wall of the canyon. On its foot-wide surface, she saw the same boot prints, some pointing down and some leading upward.

She was about to lower herself over the edge of the trail and follow that ledge path, when her ears caught the slow steady clop-clop of hoofs. A lone rider was coming up the trail. She moved swiftly up the dry wash toward Target's hiding place, trying desperately not to dislodge any telltale pebbles on the way. She had just enough time to throw herself flat near Target's feet, when the rider came in sight. She peered down at him cautiously, through the heavy brush.

Rufe Horton! The escaped prisoner!

Her hand tightened on her rifle stock. She had nearly forgotten the black-bearded horse thief. She wondered where he was going.

To her surprise, he stopped. Then he cupped his hands around his mouth. "Rufe!" he bellowed.

That was strange! He was yelling his own name! But she had another surprise coming. A moment later, another bearded face, an exact copy of his, rose up suddenly over the edge of the trail. There were two of them, as like as two peas in a pod, and each as ugly and mean-looking as the other!

She was thankful she hadn't started down that narrow ledge.

"Shut up that bellerin', Rube Horton!" the second face snarled. "You wanta let MacTavish know we're still lookin' fer him?"

Her uncle was down there somewhere! These men had been hunting him. But they hadn't found him, so she still had a chance if she could get by them! She knew very well what would happen to him if they found him first.

## 21                                  Hide and Seek

The Horton twins were arguing on the road below her hiding place, but Annie couldn't hear all of it. It ended when Rube shouted angrily, "I'm as sick of this job as you are, but we've gotta keep on lookin' fer him. Shanley an' Rango are due here any minute!"

Then they both disappeared over the edge of the trail to start the long descent to the canyon floor.

Annie ran down the dry wash this time with reckless haste. She had her rifle and six-shooter, and she would use them if she had to. Her only chance of helping Uncle Luke now was to find him, somehow, before the four could.

She started down along the narrow ledge after the twin badmen. She had no idea how far it would lead, or if she might suddenly meet one of them coming back up for some reason. But she had to keep on going.

Several times she had to hug the rough rock wall, to get over her dizziness; and once a small stone rolled under her foot, and she saved herself from a plunge only by grabbing the projecting roots of a sturdy bush.

Now she was close to the bottom. She could hear them wrangling over which was to go which way in the search. It was hot and humid down there, and neither wanted to go very far in the sun.

She waited till they were far enough away for safety, and then started her own search. There was no sound from the trail above so far. Evidently Shanley and Rango had not arrived as yet.

Her well-trained eyes soon found what she had been looking for. A wounded man had moved among these rocks, many hours ago, a man who wore high-heeled riding boots. From the depth of the imprints, he had been a heavy man, and from the size of them, a big one.

She followed his weaving trail through tangled brush and over the pebbled sand of a small dry creek. Here a growth of underbrush began, brilliantly green and lush from the waters of the little underground stream. She made her way through it, studying the ground. Here, he had stopped, perhaps to bandage his wound. Then he had gone

on, straight toward the jumbled pile of boulders at the foot
of the sloping canyon wall.

She looked up along its slope, and saw great boulders
perched there among the stunted growth of thin young
saplings. She thought uneasily, "I'm in a fine spot here,
if they decide to start sliding." She crossed her fingers the
way Tagg always did, and made a heartfelt wish that there
should be no slides till she got out from under.

She was so occupied worrying about the overhead threat
that she didn't look where she was going. Her toe caught
in the rusty head of a broken pickax on the ground, and
she fell hard on one knee. Before she could choke it off,
she had come out with a loud "Ouch!" of pain.

She heard her voice bounce against the sides of the canyon, and she cowered, gripping her rifle and fully expecting
one of the Hortons to come crashing out of the brush, gun
in hand. Instead, she heard a faint voice that was not much
more than a whisper. It came from behind the jumble of
rocks at the foot of the slope. "Annie! Over here! Quick!"

It was Uncle Luke, motioning to her now from behind
a big boulder. She got to him as quickly as she could, and
she was so happy to find him safe that she laughed and cried
at the same time, as she hugged him.

He told her that his bullet wound was not as bad as it looked, but he was bruised from his fall from the edge of the trail. He had landed in a treetop, and his six-shooter had fallen out of its holster and was lost. Later, dodging the outlaws, he had stumbled on this hiding place, the tunnel of an old abandoned Indian silver mine. Heavy underbrush and piled-up boulders made its low, timbered entrance difficult to see from even a few yards off, and the outlaws had passed it by many times last night. Fortunately, he had found a tiny trickling spring deep inside the old tunnel, and had been able to refresh himself during the long, stifling night.

"Now you're here," he told Annie, "we'll go after them. Let me have your rifle."

Annie gave him the rifle, but she told him quickly, "We've got to to get out of here right away, Uncle Luke. It's too long to explain right now, but Shanley and Rango will be here any minute to help those men gun you down."

"Shanley? Annie, what are you saying? Are you out of your mind? Those outlaws ambushed Rango and me and took Shanley's money that he trusted me to take care of!"

"They're all in it together, Uncle Luke. Those outlaws are just hired killers and Shanley's their boss!"

"She knows what she's talkin' about, Sheriff!" Rube Horton had come up behind them, a gun in his hand. "Drop the rifle, MacTavish. And you, Miss Sure Shot, don't try to go for that forty-five, or I'll blast you! Both of you get up your hands!"

There was nothing to do but obey. Annie kept her face calm, but her eyes narrowed watchfully.

Rube bellowed over his shoulder. "Hey Rufe! I got me a whole bag full! Come a-runnin'!"

Rufe's voice came from a distance. "What's that? Waddya want?"

"I want ya to come here, ya dumb—" his angry shout was choked off by a sudden deluge of sand and pebbles, that hit him square in the face from the toe of Annie's boot. His cocked six-shooter roared deafeningly as he staggered back, blinded and coughing helplessly.

Sheriff Luke grabbed up the rifle he had dropped at the badman's orders, and clouted him with it. Rube dropped like a ton of bricks, and stayed there.

But Rufe was already in sight, running and firing at them. Annie knocked his hat off with a shot. He yelped and ducked for cover.

"Hurry, Uncle Luke! Maybe we can get to the path up

the other side!" They started to run across the canyon floor, but as they did, a rifle bullet whined over their heads from the rim. They were too late. John Shanley and Rango had arrived and were taking a hand.

There was only one place to go—back into the old mine tunnel. They made a fast run for it, as fast as the sheriff, unsteady now from the wounded shoulder, could travel. Bullets sang around them as they went, from the men above and from the hidden Rufe.

At last they were inside, breathless, but safe for a moment. The sheriff had lost the heavy Springfield in the underbrush, but Annie's Colt was still in working order. She held it ready as she crouched in the darkness, out of range of the entrance, but where she could see the shadow of anyone who tried to enter.

Soon they could hear voices outside, Shanley's and Dude Rango's and the growling voices of the two Hortons. "Go in and finish them off! That's what you're getting paid for!" It was Shanley's voice.

"Try it yourself. We ain't goin' up against a dead shot like that Oakley gal!" That was one of the Hortons.

She ricocheted a shot from a boulder at the entrance. There was a yelp of pain, and a shadow moved quickly.

That was one of the Hortons, too.

"They're moving away," the tall sheriff whispered. "I don't hear their voices now."

"We'll see that they stay back," Annie answered confidently. But she was wondering where Lofty was, with the posse. What if Tagg hadn't been able to convince the men at Diablo that they should come?

"Uncle Luke, have you been far back in the tunnel? What's it look like?" She kept her voice calm.

"Gets wider. It must have been quite an important mine, in Injun times. Whole mountain's full of branch tunnels, looks like. Two or three levels, too."

"How did they get air down to the men who were working on the lower levels?"

"Same way we do nowadays . . . through an air shaft. The main one comes through from the back of this hill."

"Is it still open, do you think?" She held her breath for his answer.

"Sure is! I could see the stars through it last night, though there's brush around the openin' back there, naturally." He looked at her curiously. "What's all the questions for, honey?"

"Uncle Luke, if you feel up to some tough climbing, we

may be able to use that air shaft!" She took her gun from its holster. "But first we'll remind the boys outside to keep back!"

She moved quickly to the tunnel mouth. The four men were grouped a score or more yards away, but their voices carried clearly. She could see Rango shuffling a pack of cards. Now he spread them out like a fan, and held them out to John Shanley.

"Lowest card has to go in first," she heard him say. The Hortons and Shanley all nodded agreement.

Shanley drew a card and looked at it. Then he held it up, smiling. "An ace!" he announced.

Annie's gun barked. A hole appeared in Shanley's card. "Now it's only a two spot, Shanley, and there's nothing lower in the deck! Come on, we're waiting!" she called.

Four men scrambled to cover in four directions.

Annie retreated into the tunnel. "Let's go, Uncle Luke. I think that'll hold 'em for a few minutes."

It was a hard job getting the big sheriff up through the air shaft, but they finally did it. Annie went ahead, and when she reached the weed-grown entrance, she caught her breath and then went back down to pull and haul him through the narrow, steeply slanted passage.

They could hear the voices of the four men below, calling back and forth. They seemed to be deciding on a rush toward the mouth of the tunnel.

Sheriff Luke pointed across the canyon. "Lofty and Tagg!"

The tall young deputy and the small boy were alone. Annie realized, with a sinking heart, that no posse had come with them. Probably nobody had believed Tagg's story about the forgery.

Now the two had dismounted and Lofty was studying the four horses already tied beside the trail. Annie wanted to yell at them to warn them to go back before Shanley and Rango saw them. But she couldn't let Shanley know that she and the sheriff were safely out of the mine.

She saw Lofty and Tagg starting down the steep path along the side of the canyon. They would walk right into hot lead!

But so far the four men had not spotted them. They were sneaking up on the tunnel entrance, guns in hand. They were going to rush it. Which was just what Annie wanted them to do.

The four were waiting at the mouth of the tunnel now, guns in hand. They were probably wondering why she hadn't started shooting at them. She hoped they would think she had run out of bullets.

Now they were going in. Annie ran along the side of the hill, till she could get a clear aim at one of the giant boulders high up on the slope directly above the mine entrance. She knelt to take careful aim at a spot just under the base of the boulder.

Her bullet plowed up the dirt and sent the small rocks flying. The giant rock seemed to wobble.

Down below, Dude Rango ran out of the mine tunnel at the sound of shooting. Annie's second bullet smashed the gun out of his hand. He turned and darted back into the safety of the tunnel.

Again she fired at the heavy boulder. With a jolt, the massive thing settled down, tipped, and then went rolling and crashing down the slope, carrying with it a great rush of rocks, uprooted bushes, and sand. Above the spot where it had rested, other boulders started to slip and move, first slowly, then faster, and in a moment, a whole section of the steep slope was in motion.

Down it roared, and down, blocking the entrance of the mine tunnel, piling up rocks and debris twenty feet high on the floor of the canyon. Its rumble and crash shook the earth and echoed the length of the chasm.

As the dust settled, Annie was relieved to see Tagg and Lofty safe on the narrow pathway across the way.

"Hi, Annie!" Tagg had spotted her. "Is everything all right?"

"Just fine an' dandy!" she called back.

"What happened?" Lofty pointed down at the rock slide.

This time it was Sheriff Luke who answered, cupping his hands around his mouth. "It's a newfangled rat trap Annie made. Caught us four fine fat rats!"

"Oh!" Annie had a sudden misgiving. "Suppose they get out through the air shaft the way we did!"

"They won't," her uncle chuckled. "I plugged up the shaft with a nice sizable hunk of rock. It won't keep the air out, but it'd take more'n those four to budge it from below. They'll stay right where they are till we dig 'em out to put the handcuffs on 'em!"

## 22          Square All Around

Sheriff MacTavish's return, with Annie and Tagg and Deputy Lofty, caused a sensation. There were red faces for a while among the men who had listened to and believed John Shanley, but Luke was too honest and straightforward himself to hold it against them that they had been fooled by such a ruthless man.

John Shanley was brought to trial with his confederates, and sent to the Territorial prison for a long term. Dude Rango was glad to accept a shorter term as a reward for turning States' evidence, and the Hortons ended up on the rock pile.

The people whose money Shanley had taken illegally were repaid when the pretentious Shanley home was sold on the auction block with all its fine furnishings.

The house itself, shuttered and lonely, stood in its once

green lawns, which were now sear and dry and waist-high with rustling weeds. Edith had gone, no one knew or cared where.

Then one morning, many months afterward, the big gates swung open again, and Diablo stared open-mouthed at what they read on the big, homemade sign on the brown lawn. *Boarding House*, it said, *For Respectable Folks Only. Mr. and Mrs. David Jonathan Samuel Brewster, Props.*

And on the wide, shady veranda, Mr. Brewster rocked and rested, and Mrs. Brewster beamed and waited at his side.

Annie and Tagg were their first visitors. But there would be many others. For the Brewsters had invited all of Diablo to come and see their proudest possession, the notorious Shanley mansion, with its rose bedroom and the one with the violets, and that stuck-up Edith's bedroom, and the library where Annie had found the forgery paper. They had a star attraction here, all right. And if people got tired of just coming there to look, why, David Jonathan could always open up his barbershop in that big front hall with all the mirrors!

Later on, Annie sat on the steps of the old ranch house in the quiet evening. Tagg rested his head against her shoulder. He was half asleep already. It had been a long exciting day. Uncle Luke had won the election, practically without any opposition. He was still in town being congratulated. Since the Shanley trial, he was no longer a has-been. He would be sheriff now as long as he wanted to be. And they would be staying here on the ranch from now on, winter and summer, in peace and quiet.

She looked up at the far, quiet stars she had so often watched on the long, hard journey here, and she smiled at one in particular, bright and brilliant right above, and whispered in her thoughts, "We're really home, Mother and Dad, where you always wanted us to be, and everything's all right!"

CPSIA information can be obtained
at www.ICGtesting.com
Printed in the USA
BVHW040837070620
581005BV00011B/985